Lan

Welsh Borders

Craven Arms to Chepstow

Lawrence Garner

Published by

Landmark Publishing
Ashbourne Hall, Cokayne Ave, Ashbourne,
Derbyshire DE6 1EJ England

Lanthony Priory

Welsh Borders: Craven Arms to Chepstow

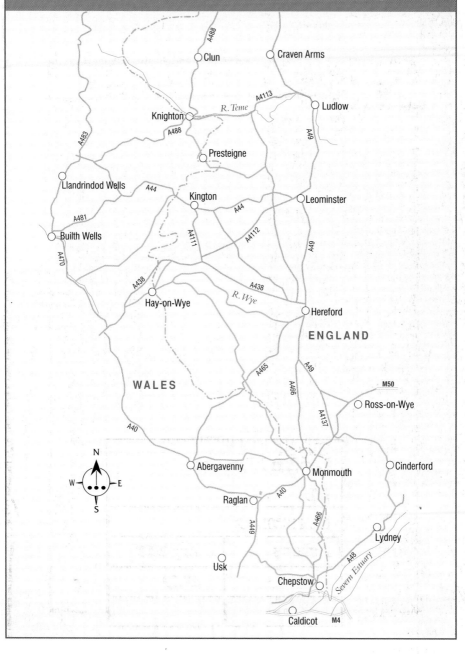

Contents

Top Tips

Tintern Abbey
Magnificent abbey remains

Hereford Cathedral
Breathtaking cathedral and the Mappa Mundi, good regional shopping centre

Raglan & Goodrich Castles
Two massive defensive castles

Ludlow town centre
Good shopping centre, old buildings and castle

Berrington Hall, nr Leominster (N.T.)
Large country mansion

Stokesay Castle (E.H.)/Shropshire Hills Discovery Centre
At Craven Arms

Hay-on-Wye
Book town and Black Mountain road to Abergavenny

Monmouth
Old county town and good for exploring areas around.

Caerwent
Roman fort – long stretches of the fort's walls survive up to 15ft (4.5m)

Offa's Dyke
It runs through a lot of scenic countryside, especially around Knighton. See map on page 38 for location of a particularly good section of the dyke

Leominster to Kington
For black & white timbered houses and cider making (south of Pembridge)

The Welsh border offers the holidaymaker more variety in a small space than any other area of Britain. Snowdonia, the Lake District, the Yorkshire Dales or East Anglia, beautiful though they are, each present one kind of landscape, which may or may not be to your taste. The Welsh border has major mountain ranges, pastoral plains, high and undulating moorland, grey towns, picturesque villages of half-timbered houses, a cathedral city, an elegant spa, rich and civilised stately homes, abandoned castles, mines and quarries, broad rivers, remote valleys, some of the most splendid churches and some of the most primitive, the richest agricultural land and the poorest.

This is the language of the holiday brochure, but it is a fact that in the course of a week here you could find yourself in half a dozen totally different environments. The reason has much to do with geography, but perhaps more to do with history.

For most of its length the border is where the plains of Cheshire, Shropshire and Herefordshire abruptly meet the upland barrier that has traditionally ensured the separate identity of Wales. A few rivers — the Usk, the Wye, the Teme, the Severn, and the Dee — have carved out the major routes through the barrier. These simple geographical

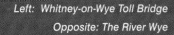

factors in themselves lead to sharp and sudden contrasts of landscape. But history has brought its own complications. I am well aware that most readers tend to skip the historical background in this sort of book, but an elementary grasp of history is necessary to understand the strange contrasts of the area.

It was fought over savagely for hundreds of years, and no British countryside has had more blood spilt on it. The people behind the Welsh hills were always a threat to whoever controlled the rich country to the east. The Romans set up border forts of varying duration, and subdued opposition with brisk efficiency, but they showed little enthusiasm for settling in the dangerous Celtic wastes. The Anglo-Saxons resigned themselves to continual border skirmishing until King Offa of Mercia constructed his famous Dyke towards the end of the eighth century and established a political border for the first time.

We know almost nothing about the reasons for the Dyke or about its construction, although new theories emerge at regular intervals. It used to be thought that it was a defensive work, but this idea has been abandoned. Most scholars see it as a simple attempt to mark out a frontier, and they doubt whether it was imposed on the Welsh by superior force. They point out that some Saxon settlements (like Buttington, near Welshpool) were left on the Welsh side, together with some very desirable farming land, and it could be that in some places the line of the Dyke was negotiated. It can even be seen as a sign of defeat for Offa — the abandonment of any hope of subduing Wales. Whatever the circumstances, it was a spectacular coast-to-coast project, stretching from Prestatyn in the north to Chepstow in the south.

Morris Men at Stokesay Castle

The establishment of a border usually has the result of encouraging nationalism, and so it proved here. Ever since the departure of the Romans in the fifth century, a distinct Celtic culture had been developing, mainly under the influence of the Celtic Church. This was the age of the 'Celtic Saints', the wandering missionaries who gave their names to so many Welsh settlements. Now came a new political awareness, and the scattered Welsh tribes began to unify under a few powerful rulers, including the legendary Princes of Powys, who controlled the central border area.

Unfortunately, while Anglo-Saxon England quietly prospered, Wales became the scene of internal struggles for power, and was in no state to meet the threat of a new enemy, the Normans. After the Conquest the border entered its bloodiest era. William the Conqueror's solution to the Welsh threat was to hand over the border to some of his most formidable followers, giving them virtual independence in return for securing his western frontier.

These great 'Marcher Lords' followed the King's example and subdivided their own territory on the same basis, and the result was a host of petty dictatorships and warring factions. The border became a battleground for some incredibly tangled warfare, pitting Welsh against Welsh, Norman against Norman, Norman against Welsh. To all intents and purposes, it was cut off from English law. The conflict was probably at its worst during the chaotic reign of Stephen, but it was not until Edward I finally gained mastery over Wales in 1282 that a semblance of peace descended.

There was still destruction to come, however. In 1400 a distinguished and civilised country gentleman named Owain Glyndwr (or Owen Glendower) was proclaimed Prince of Wales, and a desperate revolt against the English began. Glyndwr's aims were idealistic, but he showed no mercy in his campaigns, adopting 'scorched earth' tactics when necessary. His ruthlessness extended to both sides of the border, and the phrase ' laid waste by Owain Glyndwr' occurs with monotonous regularity in the guidebooks. Not until 1485 was stability established with the accession, of a Welshman, Henry VII. The Civil War of the seventeenth century was still to come.

The results of this turbulent history can be seen today. On a superficial level it explains why even insignificant hamlets have the remains of castles, although these would have been little more than wooden palisades built on earth mounds. But it also explains why, for a few miles on each side of the border, there is a distinctive sense of what can only be described as Anglo-Welshness.

It is strongest in the genuine border towns like Oswestry, Montgomery, Knighton, Kington, Presteigne and Hay-on-Wye, which survived against the odds and are still not quite sure which side they are on. The same feeling is likely to extend to anyone living west of Shrewsbury, Leominster, Ludlow or Hereford, because towns like these, far more than the political boundary, marked the beginning of England. They were securely defended and under the protection of powerful families, so that today they show all the signs of a long history of development, especially in their wealth of medieval buildings.

You will not find many medieval buildings in the corresponding Welsh towns. In fact you will find few towns of any size, and most of the buildings will be of the eighteenth century or later. Lacking protection, their growth was stunted. It is a sad fact, too, that so many of the great religious houses of the border country failed to escape the warfare and were in decline even before the Dissolution of the Monasteries. The great variety of this countryside is not, of course, entirely the result of medieval history. Simple economics have played their part. Perhaps the most striking contrast here is between the comfortable, well-developed villages of western Herefordshire, standing on rich soil, and the sparse settlements of Radnor, just across the border, where the terrain allowed only marginal subsistence for sheep. Places like Wigmore, Weobley or Pembridge are not very big but they retain the atmosphere of towns; on the Welsh side Grosmont, New Radnor and Knucklas are definitely villages that never developed, in spite of the considerable status they once had.

Here and there along the border are places that developed in surprisingly distinctive ways. The Ceiriog valley in the Berwyn mountains became a quarrying community of a kind more often found in Snowdonia, and even today it is an isolated pocket of Welshness. Oswestry became the headquarters of a big railway network. Llandrindod Wells blossomed incongruously as a Victorian spa, while Church Stretton acquired its own unique atmosphere as an Edwardian health resort. Newtown once rivalled Leeds and Bradford as a woollen town, and Craven Arms grew up as a convenient place to load sheep on to railway trucks.

It is this endless variety and power to surprise that has always attracted the discerning visitor to the border, and in recent years the area has become increasingly popular. It will never rival the Welsh coasts or Snowdonia as a tourist region, because it does not lay out its attractions. It is an intricate and rather secret landscape that has to be explored. Fortunately more and more people are becoming explorers. They are not content with lying on the beach or gazing mutely at 'beautiful scenery'. They have interests to pursue, whether it be architecture, wildlife, agriculture, industrial archeology, or simply the business of discovering the unexpected.

Within the limited scope of this book I have tried to point out some of the rewards of exploration, but I am well aware that I have only scratched the surface. It is encouraging to see that local organisations are now producing town and village 'trails', walking guides and other 'private-enterprise' literature to fill the gaps in the official tourist publications, in which the border has always been regarded as something of a no-man's-land. On reflection, perhaps that is how it should remain. As the popular holiday areas choke on their own commercialism, the Welsh border will continue to extend an unobtrusive welcome to discriminating visitors who want to create their own holiday and reject the ready-made.

Lawrence Garner
2009

1. Clun, Ludlow and the Herefordshire Border Country

The Clun Forest is well-defined and symmetrical on the map, separated from the Long Mynd range by the river Camlad, enclosed to the west by a curious bulge in the Welsh border (crazily drawn in these parts), and to the east by the Craven Arms-Knighton road. Right in the centre, at the junction of the four roads that divide the Forest into quarters, is Clun itself.

The route from Church Stretton is the A49 to **Craven Arms** and then the B4368. Craven Arms is an odd place. From the main road it seems to consist of a string of miscellaneous functional buildings, and, although there is a residential area away from the road, it did start life as a purely functional town. Situated at the junction of two railway lines, it was a convenient depot for the embarking and disembarking of enormous numbers of sheep, mainly from Wales, which were herded here for the periodic sales and then carried to all parts of the country. It still has the sales, but the sheep now travel by road. Its most distinguished building is the early 19th-century roadside hotel from which it took its name. In recent years Craven Arms has gone up in the world, and it now houses the **Shropshire Hills Discovery Centre** and an appealingly quirky **Land of Lost Content Museum** of ordinary 20th-century life. A much older attraction stands a mile or so south on the A49 – the oldest fortified house in Britain. **Stokesay Castle** is a picture-book building, but nevertheless a wholly

authentic example of a 13th-century manor house with a remarkable Great Hall.

After turning on to the B4368 at the **Craven Arms Hotel** you arrive first at **Aston-on-Clun**, an interesting village with some curious round houses and a stunted tree decked with flags. They commemorate the marriage of a local lady in the eighteenth century, although earnest scholars theorise about early pagan cults. If you have time it is worth driving the short distance to **Hopesay**, snugly situated among the hills, where the church is notable for its fine medieval roof and a wealth of carving. Hopesay Common, to the east,

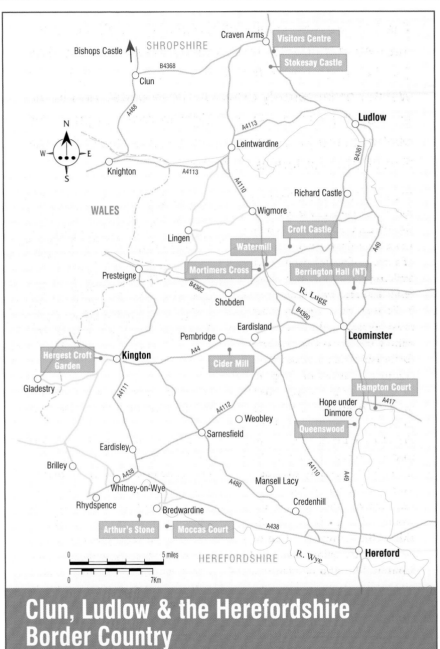

SHROPSHIRE

Bishops Castle

B4368

Clun

Craven Arms

Visitors Centre

Stokesay Castle

A488

Ludlow

N
W—E
S

Knighton

A4113

A4113

Leintwardine

B4361

A4110

Richard Castle

WALES

Wigmore

Lingen

Croft Castle

Watermill

Mortimers Cross

Presteigne

B4362

Shobden

B4360

R. Lugg

A49

Berrington Hall (NT)

Eardisland

Pembridge

Eardisland

Leominster

Hergest Croft Garden

Kington

A44

Cider Mill

Gladestry

A4111

Hampton Court

A417

Hope under Dinmore

A4112

Weobley

Sarnesfield

Queenswood

Eardisley

Brilley

A438

Whitney-on-Wye

A480

Mansell Lacy

A4110

A49

Rhydspence

Bredwardine

Credenhill

Arthur's Stone

Moccas Court

A438

R. Wye

Hereford

0   5 miles

0   7Km

HEREFORDSHIRE

Clun, Ludlow & the Herefordshire Border Country

is National Trust property and provides a pleasant short walk

This south-east quarter of the Forest is well known because of the jingle:

'Clunton, Clunbury, Clungunford
and Clun
Are the quietest places
under the sun.'

Perhaps this is the place to point out that, contrary to what every book on the area says, A. E. Housman did not write these lines, although he used them to preface one of his poems in *A Shropshire Lad*. What he did say was that this district is: *'A country for easy livers, The quietest under the sun.'* It is indeed quiet around here, but regrettably there is not much at Clunton, Clunbury or Clungunford to delay the visitor.

Clun is another matter. Its layout is typical of many small border towns that started promisingly but never developed. The original settlement is around the church on the south bank of the river, while across the bridge is the grid-patterned borough that grew up around the castle. The dominant feature of the **church** is the massive Norman tower, with a pyramid roof added in the seventeenth century, and the interior is unexpectedly rich and spacious, displaying some fine woodwork and handsome arcades. As you go out through the eighteenth-century lychgate, the town lies beneath you, with the gaunt castle away to the left. You get to it by crossing the picturesque packhorse bridge with its recesses for pedestrians. The castle is impressive not so much for its surviving ruins – mainly a three-storey keep – as for the huge earthworks around it. The town's other

main attraction is the **Holy Trinity Hospital**, a charming group of seventeenth-century almshouses with a chapel.

In the middle of the north-eastern quarter of the Forest is Lydbury North, the important centre of a very extensive manor in Saxon times. King Offa gave it to the Bishop of Hereford and his successors in the eighth century, and the new castle which the Bishop built a few miles to the west became known as Bishop's Castle, which is our next destination, reached via the A488 out of Clun.

Bishop's Castle is now a sleepy town with little sense of its former importance, which can be gauged by the fact that until 1832 it returned two MPs to Parliament, and that it survived until 1967 as Britain's smallest municipal borough. The tiny **Town Hall** still stands at the top of the High Street, complete with cells beneath, and next to it is the quaint **'House on Crutches'** – a Tudor building with one end supported on wooden posts.

Behind the Town Hall is the Castle Hotel, which has the remains of the castle in its grounds. The main street runs long and straight from here down to the church, which was largely rebuilt after suffering extensive damage during the Civil War. Other notable buildings here are Old Hall, a fine Tudor house to the east of the church, and the **'Three Tuns'**, a seventeenth-century inn with its own brewhouse next door.

The western half of the Clun Forest merges into the moorland 'desert' that stretches from Newtown in the north to Builth Wells in the south, including most of the old county of Radnorshire. It is an area of undulating hills, partly afforested, at an average height of 1500ft. To sample this remote area you can go to **Mainstone**, four miles west of Bishop's Castle, which is one of the few settlements in this part of the Forest. Its church is a mile away at Churchtown and has in it a two-hundredweight boulder, once used as a test of strength by young men of the parish. Almost due south is **Newcastle**, a rather larger place, also with a detached church and several earthworks round it. Both villages are next to Offa's Dyke, which survives for long stretches in this area; the longdistance footpath follows it closely, and forms a central 'spine' from which other walks radiate. The area to the north and west of the Clun Forest, of a very similar character, is described in later chapters. If you now want to return to Church Stretton the hills dictate that you go back the way you came. The route back to Shrewsbury from Bishop's Castle is the A488, which passes beneath the Stiperstones.

Returning to the English side of the border, this chapter is devoted to three important border towns and the countryside which they serve. Ludlow, Leominster and Hereford form a vertical line on the map, creating a natural eastern boundary to this part of the border region, where, in contrast to the Welsh side, we find pastoral valleys, rich agricultural land and picturesque villages – very much a lived-in landscape and yet strongly influenced historically by the proximity of Wales.

For many people **Ludlow** is the perfect town, with fine castle ruins, one of England's largest parish churches, a pleasing mixture of architecture, a river setting and a bustling social and cultural life. Others find it a little too self-conscious and 'arty', compared with other border towns, but no-one can deny its attractions. It is set defensively inside a bend of the river Teme with the tributary river Corve guarding its north-west side, and the old town to the west of the A49 preserves the grid pattern of a typical medieval settlement. The castle has a very close relationship with the town, symbolised by the old market square just outside the castle gates, and the whole of this central area is a cosy huddle of crowded buildings and narrow streets.

Ludlow's origins are obscure, but there was a developing community here at the end of the twelfth century with an economy based on the local wool trade, and like many wool towns its wealth was demonstrated in the size of its parish church. In the early fourteenth century the manor passed to the powerful Mortimer family, and when Edward IV (a Mortimer) was crowned king, Ludlow became a royal retreat. At various times the castle accommodated Edward V and his brother (the 'princes in the Tower'), Mary Tudor and Prince Arthur, the short-lived son of Henry VII. Arthur brought his bride Catherine of Aragon here. It is hardly surprising that, when Henry VII set up a Council of the Marches to govern Wales and the border, Ludlow was chosen as its headquarters.

In the eighteenth and nineteenth centuries, the town became the centre of a fashionable social scene, with two theatres and a racecourse, and it was during this period that the elegant Georgian houses were built. The annual Arts Festival still recaptures some of this atmosphere, and a by-pass has brought back to Ludlow something of its old tranquillity. In recent years the town has gained a widespread gastronomic reputation.

A walk around Ludlow

Ludlow demands a far more detailed exploration than can be provided here, but a brief tour of the town should start at **Castle Square**, which was originally one end of a broad main street from the castle gates to the Bull Ring beyond the church. Medieval building converted this street into a series of narrow lanes. **The castle** stands on a precipice falling away to the river and has a huge outer bailey, part of which consists of private gardens. The entrance to the inner bailey is through an Elizabethan gateway by the intimidating keep, which still has many of its interior features. The most striking building in the inner bailey is the round twelfth-century chapel, dedicated to St Mary Magdelene and revealing some fine Norman decoration. Beyond the chapel is a well-preserved range of domestic buildings; they include the Great Hall, the scene of the first performance of Milton's 'Comus' in 1634. On each side of the Hall are residential quarters where the royal visitors mentioned earlier must have lived.

It is a short walk along the High Street to **St Laurence's church**, and on the way, you pass the attractive **Buttermarket**, erected in 1746, and a fine group of fifteenth-century buildings on the corner of Broad Street. Before entering the church it is worth walking round the churchyard to see the thirteenth-century **Reader's House** and the grave of A.E. Housman, a Worcestershire man buried in the place that features so often in his poems.

Above: Broad Street, Ludlow

After passing through the hexagonal porch (an almost unique feature) you become aware at once of the cathedral-like proportions of the church, but what immediately catches the attention is the superb east window and the elaborate reredos beneath it. There is no space here for a detailed description of St Laurence's – the excellent guidebook does that well enough – but if you have time for only a quick visit you should not miss the highly individual misericords in the choir stalls or the north chancel chapel of the ancient Palmers' Guild, which has some magnificent stained glass.

In contrast to the closely-packed buildings of the High Street, **Broad Street**, leading downhill from the Buttermarket, is a spacious and elegant thoroughfare, with the Angel, a traditional coaching inn, standing out among the harmonious frontages. Running parallel to Broad Street from the castle gates is **Mill Street**, containing the **Guildhall** and the **old Grammar School**. If you turn left just beyond the school and walk through to the Broadgate you can continue on via St John's Road and emerge into Old Street, part of an ancient Roman road. At the top of Old Street is the busy junction known as the Bull Ring, and just below it stands the Feathers Hotel, featured on so many calendars and probably the best-known building in Ludlow. Built in 1603 it has an incredible profusion of decorative carving and an inviting balcony. But do not miss the Bull on the other side of the road – not so spectacular, but considerably older.

Just out of town, on the other side of the Teme bridge, there is a minor road to the right signposted '**Whitcliffe**'. This

Above: The Feathers Inn, Ludlow

leads to the common, overlooking the town, where the town's cattle grazed in the middle ages. Now it is a public area, wooded and with any number of walks, and is the start of the **Mortimer Way**, a long-distance walk south to Kington.

A circular tour of north-west Herefordshire

The tour begins and ends in Ludlow. From Ludlow take the A49 to Bromfield and turn on to the A4113 for **Leintwardine**. This is the Roman settlement of Bravonium, a long, thin village, stretched out alongside the road. Nowadays it mainly attracts fishermen, being at the confluence of the Teme and Clun, but the church is of interest because it is built on the old Roman defence works, with the result that the chancel is much higher than the nave. Less than a mile from Leintwardine you branch left on to the A4110 and soon the wooded hills on the right reveal an impressive castle mound and ruins, the first indication of the attractive village of **Wigmore**. Perhaps 'town' would be more appropriate because it was the administrative centre of northern Herefordshire for a long time, and its wide main street still gives it an air of importance. A lane leads up to the spacious church, an intriguing building with floors on different levels and with a particularly fine pulpit. A short distance to the west is an early motte and bailey, the predecessor of the much bigger castle on the outskirts that has been a bone of contention for many years because of its deterioration under private ownership. Now in the hands of English Heritage, Wigmore Castle is undergoing repair work. Parking is by the village hall, a 20 minute walk from the castle.

There is some fine hill and forest country around here, and one way to experience it is to turn right just past Wigmore and take the undulating minor road to **Lingen**. When you reach the woodland, there are plenty of opportunities for short strolls on the forest tracks. In Lingen itself there is a motte and bailey tucked away behind the farm at Court House, and the church has some interesting sixteenth-century pews, said to have come from the nearby convent at Limebrook. Turning south at the road junction in Lingen you pass a lane to the remains of the convent after a mile. It was never a big community, but the nuns were extensive landowners before the Dissolution in 1539. Another mile brings you to the river Lugg at **Kinsham**, where, just before the bridge, there is the start of a riverside walk through the gorge which the river has cut. Continue to Combe to join the B4362 and make for Shobdon, passing beneath the superb wooded ridge of Wapley Hill, which is particularly beautiful in the autumn.

Shobdon is a scattered place popular with caravanners and noted for its unusual mock-Gothic church, built in 1752 to replace a Norman church. Its plain appearance belies the fanciful extravagance of its interior. Some remains of the original church were re-erected nearby as a sort of folly. A mile or two further along the B4362, **Mortimer's Cross** is the site of a decisive battle of the Wars of the Roses in 1461. It was a triumph for Edward, Duke of York, who was crowned as Edward IV a few months later. The local pub sign shows the red and white roses and also three suns, commemorating a trick of the light on the frosty day of the battle. The main attraction here now is an eighteenth-century water-driven flour mill, a few hundred yards up the Aymstrey road.

Cross the A4110 and continue on the B4362 to reach an area of particular interest. Three miles after Mortimer's Cross is a left turn for **Croft Castle**, (National Trust) one of the few great houses in these parts open to the public. It is basically a fifteenth-century fortified mansion overlaid with later Gothic 'improvements', including a facade providing a false top storey. Inside there are some fine paintings and good furniture, some by Chippendale. It is a short walk from the rear of the castle to Croft Ambrey, the hill fort on a commanding spur overlooking the Wigmore area. The walk can be extended rewardingly by going east along the edge of the wood and then south on to **Bircher Common**, now National Trust property. The views throughout the walk are superb.

After this diversion, the road continues through the pleasant village of Bircher to join the B4361, and if you turn left you arrive at the first of several lanes leading to **Orleton**. There is a timber-framed manor house here where the poet Pope once stayed and a Norman church with a particularly fine carved font. The final stop before re-entering Ludlow is at **Richard's Castle**. The modern village by the road is undistinguished and you need to travel a mile up a side road to the west to see the site of one of the very earliest Norman castles, probably founded before the Conquest by Richard le Scrob, who gave his name to the village. Nearby is the old church, rarely used now, with a detached tower and seventeenth-century box pews. The new church, close to the main road, is also worth visiting, being the work of the distinguished Victorian architect Norman Shaw.

On to Leominster and central Herefordshire

To explore the central border area of Herefordshire we take the A49 (Leominster) road out of Ludlow. About three miles after Brimfield there are signs for **Berrington Hall**, an important National Trust property standing in an extensive park laid out by Capability Brown. The house was built during the period 1778-1781 for Thomas Harley, a former Lord Mayor of London. Its severe, rectangular exterior contains a wealth of elegant decoration and furnishing, and the showpiece of the house is the staircase hall, a masterpiece by the architect Henry Holland.

As you arrive at **Leominster** (pronounced Lemster) you should avoid being caught in its one-way system by taking advantage of the large car park on the left soon after you enter the town from the north. As a town, Leominster has been overshadowed by its grander neighbours, Ludlow and Hereford, but many visitors will find its intimate atmosphere and general homeliness more appealing. In fact, it has much in common with its rivals, including a parish church on the grand scale, a medieval centre and some good Georgian architecture.

It is the latter that first becomes noticeable as you approach the town centre from the car park. **Broad Street** lives up to its name, and has some pleasing eighteenth-century buildings that function in an unassuming way as shops and offices. At the top of Broad Street you reach the semi-pedestrianised heart of the old town, with a wealth of timber-framed buildings in **High Street** and **Draper's Lane**. Much of the ancient beauty of these buildings has been lost at ground level because of the modernisation of shop-fronts, but the first floors show a fascinating variety of styles. **Corn Square**, at the other end of Draper's Lane, is the site of the town's open-air Friday market, and beyond is Etnam Street, containing a mixture of Georgian and timber-framed architecture. Church Street leads off from the top of Broad

Left: Croft Castle, near Mortimer's Cross, from the walled garden

Below: The watermill at Mortimer's Cross

Below: The Priory, Leominster

Street, displaying some handsome eighteenth and nineteenth-century houses. It takes you to the **Priory Church of St Peter and St Paul**, which is not only a unique building in itself but a reminder that the town's origins were ecclesiastical.

The first religious community was probably founded here in about 660 and was the spiritual centre for a very wide area before Hereford Cathedral was built to take over that role. Successive communities did not run smoothly, and in 1123 Leominster Priory was put under the jurisdiction of Reading Abbey. It was at this time that work was begun on rebuilding the Priory Church, and the Norman nave is readily identifiable by its massive pillars and the fact that it is on a lower level than the rest of the church. An aisle on its left contains, rather incongruously, the town's ducking stool for scolds. This original portion was dedicated to St Peter, whereas the central nave, built in 1239 for the benefit of the townspeople, is dedicated to St Paul. To the south is a huge aisle which is virtually a third nave. It was added in 1320 in the elegant 'decorated' style, with a set of magnificent windows. Originally the church was about twice its present length, but the choir, presbytery and Lady Chapel, which made up the east end, were destroyed at the Reformation.

There is one other important building in Leominster, reached by going south through the churchyard gate into the neighbouring park. The splendid, timber-framed **Grange**, built in 1633, originally stood in the town centre, serving as the town hall and market. The builder was John Abel, Herefordshire's master-craftsman in timber-framing, whose name will occur again later. It was moved to its present site in 1856, and although the ground floor has now been filled in it remains one of the county's best traditional buildings.

Around the Arrow valley

This circular tour of the Arrow valley begins on the A4112 out of Leominster. After about three miles there is a right turn on to the A44, from which a lane leads to **Eardisland**. If a Hollywood set-designer had been given the task of creating an English village he would probably have come up with something like Eardisland. An old bridge spans a narrow river whose banks are immaculate lawns. Gleaming black-and-white cottages group themselves picturesquely around it, a mellow brick dove-cot is in the middle distance and a mill stream winds its way through. Only the thatch is missing. The **church of St Mary the Virgin** is not exceptional, apart from a fine modern stained-glass window showing Christ as the Good Shepherd with black-and-white houses in the background. The dovecot is open to the public. Possibly of late seventeenth-century date, it is a square, two-storey brick structure with a four-gabled roof, built on two storeys. The lower room was apparently designed for occupation, and between 1869 and 1874 housed a school for girls. The actual dovecot space above now houses a collection of Automobile Association memorabilia. One of Eardisland's most interesting buildings stands by the bridge. The oldest section of **Staick House** (not open to the public) is fourteenth century, and extensions were built in the two succeeding centuries. Its roof is a good example of sandstone slab cladding.

A turning to the left after the bridge will bring you to **Burton Court**, which is open to the public. It is mainly of the late eighteenth century with later additions, among them a porch by Clough Williams Ellis of Portmeirion fame. The oldest part of the house is a fourteenth-century Great Hall. Extra interest is provided by a collection of models, curios and items of period costume.

Return to the A44 and continue to **Pembridge**, which is as picturesque as Eardisland but rather less self-conscious, with timber-framed houses lined up solidly on each side of the road. The natural focus of the village is half-way along the main street, where the church, the **market hall** and the New Inn form an interesting group. The inn is seventeenth century and perhaps over-restored, but the early sixteenth-century market hall, with its open ground floor, is of interest because it is the only single-storey timber-framed example in the county. Its supporting oak timbers still show the notches that held the merchants' stalls in position over three hundred years ago. The steps to the churchyard are opposite, and it comes as a slight shock to be confronted with an almost grotesque detached belfry, squat and massive. It was obviously built to serve also as a fortress, and the bullet holes in the door are said to be from the Civil War. By contrast, the **church of St Mary**, rebuilt in the fourteenth century, has an atmosphere of elegance and richness, and its size is a reminder that Pem-

bridge was once an important borough. There are unusual carved panels on the pulpit and lectern. In Bridge Street the **Duppa Almshouses**, endowed by a seventeenth-century Bishop of Winchester and still in use, form a charming group, with their stone roof and big chimneys. A feature of Pembridge is the number of **cruck houses**. This form of building, in which the timbers are fastened to giant, curved A-frames at each end of the house, is widespread in Herefordshire. The Forge and Victoria Place in East Street are examples.

The A44 continues into **Kington**, standing in the shadow of Hergest Ridge. By a process common in the border country, the original settlement at the top of the hill has been outstripped by later development below it. Like several towns we have encountered before it makes no claim to be anything but a useful rural centre with modest streets and no outstanding architecture, although the Burton Arms, opposite the market hall is a remarkably attractive mid-Victorian building, while behind the market hall a restoration project has produced the Old Coach House, built on brick piers and housing the public conveniences.

At the west end of the town is a tall clock tower commemorating Queen Victoria's Golden Jubilee in 1887. Next to it is Kington's **museum**, housing displays of local interest. **St Mary's church** stands high on a hill, with a Norman tower and a distinctive three-decker spire. The rest of the church is something of a conglomeration of alterations and additions. The principal feature is the tomb in the south chancel of Thomas Vaughan and his wife, known as 'Black Vaughan' and 'Ellen the Terrible'. They lived at Hergest Court nearby, and their nicknames give some indication of their reputation. Ellen is reputed to have avenged the murder of her brother by dressing as a man, taking part in an archery tournament and killing the murderer with her first shot. Opposite the church the old **Grammar School** was endowed in 1632 by Lady Margaret Hawkins, the wife of Admiral Sir John Hawkins, and built by John Abel. There are some attractive old cottages below the church on the other side, and down the road beyond them is the track of an early nineteenth-century horse tramway, part of a system that extended to Lyonshall, Eardisley and Hay.

It is fairly easy to explore the high ground around Kington on foot by following sections of the Offa's Dyke path. **Rushock Hill** is a worthwhile objective because the path goes by Bradnor Hill, a noted viewpoint. To reach the path you turn off Church Street at the Swan Inn, turn left into Common Close, and continue past the national school to a footbridge over the Back Brook. The path crosses the golf course, one of several claiming to be the highest in Britain, and after two miles or so reaches Rushock Hill, where there is a good surviving stretch of Dyke. By taking the Dyke path in the opposite direction it is possible to get on to **Hergest Ridge**, which also provides magnificent views. Pass the church and take the turning to the left signposted 'Ridgebourne/Hergest Croft'. At the end of the lane is a gate giving access to the path, which can be followed all the way to Gladestry.

The name Hergest (pronounced 'Hargest', with a hard 'g') figures largely in this area. Hergest Croft, with its celebrated gardens, is open to the public. It should not be confused with Hergest Court, which is not open but which is of great significance in Welsh cultural history. Nowadays it looks like a rather elaborate farmhouse, a mile from Kington on the Gladestry road, but it is immediately noticeable since it stands on high ground across a small valley. Two of the most famous collections of Welsh folk-tales, the Red and White Books of Hergest, were preserved here. The White Book was destroyed by fire in 1808, but the Red Book was translated from old to modern Welsh and then translated into English by Lady Charlotte Guest as *The Mabinogion* .

From Kington the tour continues on the A4111 south to **Eardisley**. Since it is a long, straggling place, stretched out along the main road, it does not have the intimate atmosphere of some other Herefordshire villages; but some of its buildings deserve attention. The **Tram Inn** is a reminder of the railway from Kington mentioned earlier, and just around the corner from it is a small cruck cottage. The Forge in the main street is also of cruck construction. But one of the most attractive buildings is close to the church – a conversion of an old timber-framed barn into a terrace of four cottages. Also close to the church is the mound of a castle that was once extremely important. An unpopular thirteenth-century Bishop of Hereford was imprisoned here after a long record of extortion on behalf of Henry III and himself. The showpiece of the **church of St Mary Magdalene** is its remarkable Norman font, carved with the

Above: The early sixteenth century Market Hall and the New Inn, Pembridge

Left: Hergest Croft garden

Above: Weobley

figures of a lion, two people fighting and a traditional 'harrowing of Hell'. Like so much of the church carving in Herefordshire, it conveys a sense of enjoyment in the craftsman rather than just a sense of duty, and scholars have been able to identify a definite style among these local craftsmen, who have come to be known as the Herefordshire School of Carving.

You turn on to the A4112 at Eardisley for the return to Leominster, and the first stop for anyone interested in architecture will be at **Sarnesfield**. Beside the church porch here is the tomb of John Abel, the master builder, who died in 1674 at the age of 97. He carved the tomb himself, including on it his wives as well as the tools of his trade. Many examples of his work have now been demolished, but the Grange at Leominster still stands, as does the old Grammar School at Kington and the roof and screen of Abbey Dore.

Soon after leaving Sarnesfield, the lofty spire of the church at **Weobley** appears on the right. This small town has been by-passed, and is a pleasant place for a leisurely stroll without intrusive traffic. On closer inspection, the spire is obviously something of a status symbol, being out of proportion to the rest of the church, and indeed Weobley was once one of the county's biggest and wealthiest boroughs, being specially noted for its ale. One of its most famous figures was Colonel John Birch, the Parliamentary leader, who was MP for the town and settled here after the Restoration. His striking memorial is next to the altar in the church.

Weobley (pronounced Webley) is rightly celebrated as the gem of Herefordshire's 'black and white villages', and it is impossible here to give a detailed account of it. The focal point, simply because the wide street suddenly narrows there, is the Red Lion, a fine building in itself but also hiding at its back a superb example of a cruck-framed house. The spacious air of the upper main street is partly the result of a fire which burned down an island of buildings in 1860 (they included John Abel's market hall), and a garden has now replaced them. Not all the buildings are medieval, of course, and there are examples here of the widespread habit in the border counties of painting 'beams' on to whitened brick houses. Elsewhere in Britain this would be condemned as fakery, but here it can be seen as a mark of respect. The old Grammar School is one later structure (c. 1660) which can compete with its older neighbours. If you are not overwhelmed by timber-framing after a walk round Weobley, it is worth the short journey south-west to the Ley (1589), one of the best timber-framed buildings in the county. **Dilwyn**, with its fine church, is the last stop before the return to Leominster.

On to Hereford

The parts of Herefordshire we have explored so far are associated with two rivers, the Lugg and the Arrow. The third and most famous of the county's rivers is the Wye, and to reach it you turn south from Leominster and make for Hereford. This stretch of the A49 is of little interest except at Dinmore Hill, where the road climbs in striking fashion through woodland. **Hope**

under Dinmore, at the bottom of the hill, is an example of a village thoughtlessly divided by road 'improvements' which have left the church and the school isolated from the village. The stately home to the east of Hope is **Hampton Court**, a house of great architectural interest as a rare example of a fortified fifteenth-century manor, built round a courtyard with a gatehouse. Built by Sir Roland Lenthall with money acquired during the Agincourt campaign, it was bought by the Earl and Countess of Coningsby, whose family later sold it to Richard Arkwright, son of the inventor. The Coningsbys' young son died in 1708 after choking on a cherry, and on a memorial in Hope church he is shown holding the fatal fruit. An ancestor founded the Coningsby Hospital in Hereford.

The house remains private, but the gardens have recently been opened to the public, and, among many other attractions, feature a yew-tree maze with a gothic tower at its centre and a conservatory designed by Joseph Paxton. You can also visit another part of the original estate by driving to the top of the hill to the entrance on the right. This is the former Dinmore Hill wood, acquired by the County Council in 1935. Since then an arboretum has been developed, and now it has become the 170-acre **Queenswood Country Park**. There are specimens of over four hundred varieties of trees as well as a large area of oak woodland. A whole network of paths makes for pleasant walking, and the Queen's View looks out over a magnificent panorama from the Malvern Hills to the Black Mountains.

There is another outdoor attraction at **Bodenham**, reached by a lane on the left shortly after the entrance to the Queenswood Country Park. The **Bodenham Lake Nature Reserve** includes over 100 acres of varied habitat, plus the largest area of open water in the county, formed from old gravel pits. Bodenham itself is a 'typically English' village, and untypical of Herefordshire in that it is grouped round a small village green, with a church whose small spire sits oddly on top of a large tower. In the spacious interior there is a mysterious medieval monument showing a woman and child. After Dinmore Hill the road drops sharply towards Hereford with the Lugg valley on the left. Just before entering the city you cross the line of a Roman road at **Holmer**, which has a church with a detached tower and fine roof timbers.

The first problem in the city itself is where to park the car, and you penetrate its complex road system at your peril. As you enter the city from this direction you will pass the Hereford United football ground on your left. Keep left at the next roundabout and look out for the Market car parks on the left shortly afterwards.

A walk around Hereford

From the Market car park you can walk into Widemarsh Street, which contains two of Hereford's historic attractions. The **Coningsby Hospital** is a group of almshouses founded for the benefit of old soldiers in 1614 by a member of the Coningsby family of Hampton Court at Dinsmore. The foundation is reputed to have led local girl Nell Gwynne to urge Charles II to establish the Royal Hospital, Chelsea. The building now houses tableaux and exhibits commemorating this aspect of its history, and there is also a small museum concerned with the Knights of St John of Jerusalem, whose hospice and chapel it had been. The secluded **Blackfriars Gardens** are next door. They are all that remain of the monastery, but they contain a fourteenth-century preaching cross that is believed to be unique.

Widemarsh Street is the most direct route to the town centre. Once you are over the ring road you become aware of the homely timber-framed buildings and small-scale architecture that characterises the city – a rather grandiose term for what is essentially a large market town. You emerge into **High Town**, with a large pedestrianised area to the left, but if you turn right you will arrive after a few yards at the ancient church of **All Saints**, with its twisted spire. Apart from being a beautiful building in itself, with notable choir stalls, it houses a chained library of three hundred books – the second largest in England (the largest is in the Cathedral). A presumptuous nineteenth-century churchwarden sold the lot to a dealer for £100, and the church authorities intervened just in time to prevent the sale. Although still in use for worship, All Saints now serves as a community activity centre and has a popular café.

Moving back to High Town, the lively hub of the city's shopping area, you will see at the far end a Jacobean house, looking oddly marooned like a ship in dry dock. This is the **Old House**, once part of a street called Butcher's Row and now preserved as a museum

of seventeenth-century furniture and household effects. The Old House is the last survivor of the buildings that once crowded this former market square. The greatest of all, and reckoned to have been the finest timber-framed building in Europe, was the vast Guildhall, unthinkably demolished in 1862. On the evidence of old prints it was a breathtaking building. Red stones have been set into the paving of the precinct to mark the position of its piers.

Immediately behind the Old House is **St Peter's**, another of Hereford's medieval churches. Originally founded in 1074, it became a priory church in 1100 and a parish church in 1131, its demotion being due to the completion of the Cathedral. The building in classical style on the other side of St Peter's Square is the **Shire Hall**, designed by Robert Smirke in the early nineteenth century. St Owen's Street leads away from St Peter's Square, and contains some distinguished Georgian architecture; it is also a convenient route to the site of the castle, which is reached by turning right into Cantelupe Street. **Castle Green** stands high above the river. There are no remains of the castle itself apart from nearby Castle Cliffe, a building that has had many uses. It was the Governor's house during the Civil War, later became the county gaol and is now a holiday home. The monument in the middle of Castle Green, incidentally, is the local Nelson's Column, erected in 1809.

From Castle Green it is possible to cross the river by the Victoria footbridge and admire the view of the Cathedral as you walk through Bishop's Meadow to the **Old Wye Bridge**, which dates from 1100. It is difficult

Left: Hereford Cathedral

*Below: The Mappa Mundi
in Hereford Cathedral, the
largest medieval map in
existence, dating from c. 1300*

*Reproduced by kind permission of the
Dean and Chapter of Hereford*

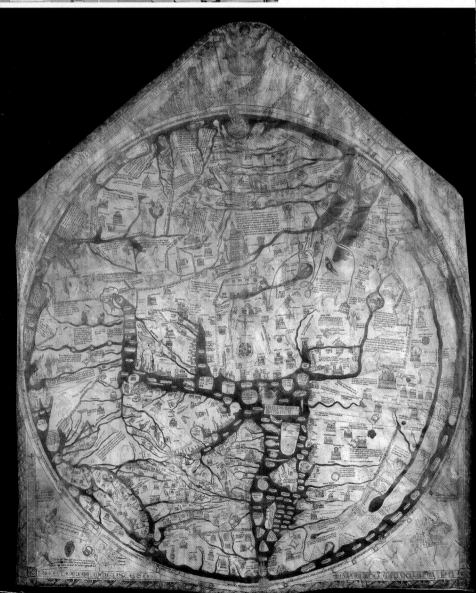

Above: Hampton Court Gardens

Above: The Old House, Hereford

now to believe that this bridge carried all traffic in and out of the city until 1967. On the other side of the bridge, the first turning on the right takes you into **Gwynne Street**, where a plaque marks Nell's birthplace, and, if you continue through Palace Yard, you confront **Broad Street**, Hereford's most impressive thoroughfare.

There are two eye-catching buildings here – the splendid Green Dragon Hotel and the spectacular gothic frontage of the **city library and museum**, well worth visiting for its permanent collection and its temporary exhibitions. Other notable buildings here include the former town house of the Duke of Norfolk opposite the hotel and, at the bottom on the right, St Xavier's Roman Catholic Church. All Saints church and spire closes off the end of the street as you look up it.

Now to the **Cathedral**. Tradition claims that Hereford has had a bishop since the seventh century (although he probably had a roving commission and was not resident) and it is likely that the first Cathedral was erected in about 730. Nothing remains of this building or of anything before the Norman Conquest; the present Cathedral seems to have been started in 1080 and has been added to ever since. The whole structure is now beautifully maintained, but it was not always so. On Easter Monday 1786 there was a catastrophe when the west tower fell, destroying part of the nave. In his book *The River Wye* Keith Kissack gives an entertaining account of this and other near-disasters, quoting the Hereford Journal's casual comment that 'the ruins, though awful, afford a pleasing view, especially to behold the

statues of kings and bishops resting one upon the other'.

The next fifty years saw half-hearted and muddled attempts at restoration, done as cheaply as possible and in poor taste. It was during this period that the Cathedral came close to losing its priceless chained library of over 1400 books. In 1842 they were stored in a lumber room, and the Dean of the time warned that unless they were shifted the 'rubbish' would be burnt! The library is now safely housed in a new building at the west end and is open to visitors, along with the Cathedral's main treasure, the famous **Mappa Mundi**, a 700-year-old Map of the World, drawn in the late thirteenth century. The map shows the Garden of Eden, Noah's Ark, Lot's Wife, the Sphinx and the Pillars of Hercules as well as more factual information. The shrine of St Thomas of Hereford in the north transept is a reminder of the last of the pre-Reformation English saints. Thomas de Cantilupe was Bishop here from 1274 to 1282, and after he had died in Italy his bones were brought back to Hereford. After hundreds of reports of miracles at his tomb, he was canonised in 1307. The finest architecural feature of the Cathedral is perhaps the exquisite Lady Chapel.

Between the Cathedral and the river are two further places of interest. The detached **Bishop's Palace** has a bland Victorian air, concealing the fact that it may well be the oldest domestic timber-framed building in England, with a hall dating from the late twelfth century. At the south-east end of the Cathedral are the fifteenth-century former lodgings of the College of Vicars Choral, minor orders among the cathedral staff.

You can return to Widemarsh Street and the car by walking up the pleasant shopping lane called Church Street, which leads away from the north front of the Cathedral. You will not have exhausted Hereford's attractions, however. There is a whole riverside area, recalling that the city was once a thriving river port and shipbuilding town.

The south Herefordshire countryside – a circular tour

There is some attractive countryside west of Hereford, much of it dominated by the river Wye. The A438 out of the city brings you after about four miles to King's Acre, after which you branch right on to the A480. **Credenhill** is remembered because of its associations with the poet Thomas Traherne, who became Rector here in 1652 after starting life in Hereford as the son of a shoemaker. Oddly enough, the son of another Rector of Credenhill also made history in a way; HP Bulmer started making cider here before moving his business into Hereford in 1887. The village itself is unremarkable, but the church has some good fourteenth-century stained glass. The church is also the showpiece of Brinsop, containing as it does some of the best work of the Herefordshire School of Carvers, as well as a fourteenth-century rood screen and some fine glass. The memorials in the church indicate that the local squires were the Daunseys of Brinsop Court. Wordsworth frequently stayed

here when visiting his wife's brother, and it would be interesting to know what he made of this moated manor-house, 600 years old and looking well today. **Mansell Lacy** is tucked away off the main road, and most tourists stop only long enough to photograph the half-timbered post office with its dove-cot, but it is worth lingering to admire the buildings of what seems an enviable place in which to live.

You now move into an area covered earlier in the chapter, and it is best to turn left on to the minor road at Calver Hill and make for the A438 again. But before turning back towards Hereford along the Wye valley, you should carry on as far as **Rhydspence**, which is not really a village but an inn. You can hardly miss it, as it stands in a commanding position by the road. Dating from the sixteenth century, it was once known simply as the Cattle Inn because it was an important staging post for drovers as they brought their beasts from Wales to the English markets. There were shoeing facilities here for the oxen, but equally important were the drinking facilities, and the Revd Francis Kilvert notes in his famous Diary that noise and singing often went on well into the night.

At the bottom of the hill below Rhydspence is a turning for **Brilley**. It is a long climb through a scattered village with some interesting early houses, but as you level out at the top there is a National Trust signpost marked **Cwmmau Farmhouse**. The narrow road leads down to an area of common with views over the Wye, and a little way beyond is the farmhouse itself. It has been preserved by the Trust as an example of a traditional Herefordshire farmhouse, with timber-framing and stone roof-cladding. Unfortunately, it is open freely to the public only at Easter and on certain bank holidays, although a private visit can be arranged in advance by writing to the occupier. It is worth taking the trouble because so much of the county's architecture can only be admired from the outside, whereas at Cwmmau the building techniques can be studied in detail.

There is now a choice of routes back to Hereford on either side of the river, and the lack of bridges makes it difficult to move from one to the other. Perhaps the best compromise is to take the A438 to Letton and then turn right for **Bredwardine**, where the diarist Francis Kilvert ended his days. He was 39 when he died from peritonitis a few weeks after his marriage in 1879. His tomb is in the churchyard. Bredwardine itself is a pleasant village with a church containing several Norman features, an attractive inn and the remains of a castle next to the church. Its fine six-arched bridge is one of the few along this stretch of the river to have survived frequent severe floods in the past. There is a chance here to walk up above Bredwardine and see **Arthur's Stone**, an ancient burial chamber. At the crossroads by the Red Lion take the Moccas road, then the first turning to the right towards **Dorstone**. Turn right after about a mile on to a lane which passes the Stone. As you face south here, you are at the head of the Golden Valley, described in the next chapter. Continue down on the same lane, turning right at the junction. **Moccas Court**, now a hotel, is a little way along the river. It is a classic eighteenth-century house and very elegant indeed, with a beautiful circular drawing room decorated unusually with French paper panels. Adjacent is **Moccas Park**, now a National Reserve, protecting huge and ancient oaks.

It is a good idea to stay on this side of the river in order to visit the church at **Madley**, which is noted for its unusual size and splendour (the font is said to be the second largest in England). It was a considerable place of pilgrimage in the fourteenth century, and most of it dates from that time. The east window has some medieval stained glass, although this is outshone by the glass at **Eaton Bishop**, four miles away. The return to Hereford is over the new Wye Bridge, which is the starting point for the next chapter of this guide.

Below: Moccas Park Reserve

Places to Visit

Craven Arms

Shropshire Hills Discovery Centre

Craven Arms SY7 9RS
☎ 01588 676000
Open: daily
Family events

Stokesay Castle (E.H)

SY7 9AH
7 miles NW of Ludlow off A49
☎ 01588 676000
Open: Apr–Sep daily 10am-5pm.
Reduced opening in winter
Family events.
Finest fortified Medieval manor house in England.

Clun Forest

Clun Castle (English Heritage)

Substantial three-storey keep,surrounded by massive earthworks. Open access.

Clun Museum

In the Town Hall.
Local history and life.

Walcot Hall

At Lydbury North, 7 miles north-east of Clun.
☎ 01588 680570
30 acres of garden and arboretum, with walks and fishing pools.

Bury Ditches

Roadside car park on A488 north of Clun. Iron Age fort with elaborate defences. Forestry Commission picnic site with walks and cycle trails.

Ludlow

Tourist information

At Ludlow Museum, Castle Square.
☎ 01584 813666

Ludlow Castle

Of great significance in English history. Very extensive remains, including keep, chapel, gatehouse and residential quarters.

Parish Church of St Laurence

☎ 01584 872073
One of the largest in the country, mostly re-built in the mid-15th century but some earlier features survive. Fine misericords and stained glass. The poet A.E. Housman is commemorated in the churchyard.

Ludlow Assembly Rooms

Mill Street
☎ 01584 878141
Arts centre providing cinema, music, and drama.

Ludlow Museum

Castle Street
☎ 01584 873857
Exhibitions from the building on the castle to the 18th century. Also `Reading The Rocks': a celebration of Ludlow's contribution to international geology.

Places to Visit

Linney Riverside Park

Boats for hire, putting green and a children's play area.
Below Ludlow Castle.

Whitcliffe Common

Steep, wooded area overlooking castle and river. Short walks, two geological sites of Special Scientific Interest.

Feathers Inn

Bull Ring
Famous 'picture postcard' demonstration of elaborate timber framing.

Leominster

Tourist Information

1 Corn Square
☎ 01568 616460

Priory church

Large, unique church of outstanding architectural interest.

Folk Museum

16 Etnam Street
☎ 01568 615186
Displays of local life in the past.

The Grange

In park adjacent to churchyard. former town hall by master carpenter John Abel. One of the finest half-timbered buildings in the county.

Berrington Hall (National Trust)

On A49, 3 miles north of Leominster.
☎ 01568 615721
Open: mid-Mar–end-Oct, Sat-Wed. Splendid 18th- century mansion with much original decoration and fine furniture. Dairy and Victorian laundry, gardens.

Burton Court,

At Eardisland, 6 miles west of Leominster.
☎ 01544 388231
Eighteenth-century house with nineteenth-century additions. 14th-century Great Hall. Special displays, costume collection.

Croft Castle (National Trust)

On B4362, 4 miles northwest of Leominster
☎ 01568 780246
Open: Apr–end-Oct, Wed–Sun, also weekends in Mar.
Fine country house with walls and fortifications of 14th and 15th centuries. Main house of sixteenth century with 'Gothic' additions. Very attractive grounds.

Mortimers Cross Watermill (English Heritage)

7 miles north-west of Leominster on B4362.
Rare one-man-operated 18th-century water mill in part working order. Attractive gardens and woodland walks nearby.

Hampton Court

Off A49 at Hope under Dinmore.
☎ 01568 797777
Manor house, originally of 15th century. Famous gardens have now been restored. Many unusual features. Restaurant.

Queenswood Arboretum and Country Park

Dinmore Hill, Leominster HR6 0PY
☎ 01568 798320
Open: daily, dawn–dusk.
Wide range of rare and unusual trees, including collection of Californian redwoods and avenue of 40 different species of oak.

Bodenham Lake Nature Reserve

Off A49, 2 miles south of Hope under Dinmore
Former gravel pits, now reserve with varied habitats. Riverside meadows, orchards, woodland. Lake is the largest area of open water in Herefordshire.

Kington

Tourist Information

2 Mill Street
☎ 01544 230778

Kington Muceum

Mill Street, Kington
☎ 01544 231486
Open: Apr–Sep, 10.30am-4pm.
Devoted to local history and the life of the community.

Hergest Croft Gardens

On western outskirts of Kington
☎ 01544 230 160
Open: Apr–Oct, daily noon-5.30pm, Mar Sat-Sun noon-5.30pm.
Celebrated gardens with magnificent views. Hidden valleys, woodland glades, open parkland, contained in four distinct gardens covering 50 acres. Tea room, shops.

Oaklands Small Breeds Farm and Owl Centre

At Kingswood, Kington
☎ 01544 231109
Farm park with many additional attractions, ideal for children.

Kinnersley Castle

At Kinnersley, 8 miles south of Kington on A4112.
☎ 01544 327 875
Former Marcher castle, now basically Elizabethan mansion built for the Vaughan family. Fine interior features, including 16th-century plasterwork. Attractive grounds, interesting Norman church adjacent.

Pembridge

Westonbury Mill Water Gardens

Off the A44 between Leominster and Kington.
☎ 01544 388650
Open: The gardens are open seven days a week from Apr–end-Sep 11am to 5pm.

Places to Visit

Hereford

Tourist Information

1 King Street
☎ 01432 268430

Hereford Cathedral

Superbly positioned, noted for Early English Lady chapel, shrine of St Thomas of Hereford, and chained library.

The Chained Library

At Hereford Cathedral.
☎ 01432 374200
1500 books - the largest chained library in the world. Very early manuscripts, including 8th-century Hereford Gospels. The New Library Building, in the cathedral cloisters also contains the Mappa Mundi, a unique 13th-century map of the world.

Hereford Museum and Art Gallery

Broad Street, Hereford.
☎ 01432 260692
Open: daily Tue-Sat, 10am-5pm (4pm Sun in summer). Free.
Spectacular Victorian building, housing local history displays.

All Saints Church

High Street, Hereford
☎ 01432 370414
Interesting medieval church, now doubling as community centre with highly-regarded restaurant.

Blackfriars Rose Garden

In Widemarsh Street
Secluded oasis contains the remains of the friary of the Blackfriars.

Coningsby Hospital and Museum

In Widemarsh Street
☎ 01432 274903
Open: Easter–Oct Wed-Sat 11am-3pm.
Almshouses of c. 1614, with adjacent museum relating to Knights Hospitallers of St. John of Jerusalem.

Hereford Cider Museum

21 Rylands Street, Hereford.
☎ 01432 354207
Open: Apr–Oct 10am-5pm, Nov–Mar 11am-3pm.
Story of traditional cider making, with reconstructed farm cider house, machinery, artefacts and ephemera.

Hereford Waterworks Museum

Broomy Hill, Hereford.
☎ 01432 344062
Open: Easter–Oct Tues 11am-5pm. Also 2nd last Sun in each month 2-5pm.
Devoted to history of drinking water, with array of pumping engines. Children's trail.

2. Radnor and the central Welsh Border

Below: Bleddfa

This chapter explores the border area south of Newtown, an area that approximates to the old county of Radnorshire, now part of Powys.

Although tourism has been encouraged in recent years, it remains a little-known part of mid-Wales, and not much has been done to change the characteristic appearance of this sparsely-populated area. It is a countryside of bare, undulating hills and moorland, with frequent higher and more massive ranges and sudden sharp ridges. As you move through it the hills constantly assume new patterns in a confusing way. It is fine walking country, but to be treated with caution. Like much border hill country it appears perfectly safe until you take a wrong turning, when the absence of prominent landmarks or human habitation can be disconcerting. A sixteenth-century writer said of Radnorshire: *'The air thereof is sharp and cold for that the snow lieth and lasteth long unmelted under the shadowing high hills and overhanging rocks. The soil is hungry, rough and churlish and hardly bettered by painful labour'*. Not surprisingly the economy of Radnor has been traditionally based on sheep, although in recent years forestry has become an important factor.

South from Newtown

As you move south from Newtown on the A483 you are aware at once of being in a different kind of country. The road climbs steadily through a series of tortuous bends, and the Severn valley gradually disappears from view. After about six miles the road winds in spectacular fashion round Glog Hill, and shortly afterwards the river Ithon appears on the right. The first village of any size is **Llanbadarn Fynydd**. It is unremarkable in itself, but is the centre of a network of walks (clearly shown on the OS map) offering expeditions of any length and variety. From the point of view of clothing and protection, you need to bear in mind that you are at a thousand feet before you start climbing. Convenient access to the hills is by way of the lane leading north-east out of Llanbadarn.

Three miles south of the village you pass on the left a picnic place and some thoughtfully-sited toilets. This is a good place to stop because a hundred yards further on, nestling under the road to the right, is the church of **Llananno**. In the subsequent chapters there will be many references to rood-screens, but Llananno is reckoned to have the finest in Wales. It is a miracle of fifteenth-century carving, and equally miraculous is the fact that it was carefully replaced when the church was restored in the nineteenth century. Its origin is uncertain, but according to tradition it came from the abbey at Cwmhir, further south.

Very soon after Llananno comes the sizeable village of **Llanbister**, now bypassed by the main road, but worth turning off for, in order to see another rare piece of church architecture, an eighteenth-century choir loft with a tiny schoolroom below. The main features of interest at **Llandewi Ystradenny**, four miles further on, are the twin hill forts to the north. They can be reached on foot by a track to the left of the main road about a quarter of a mile before the village centre. It is a steep but satisfying walk.

Half a mile beyond Llandewi the road

crosses the Ithon, and the bridge is a good starting point for a walk to the ruins of the famous **Abbey Cwmhir**. The route starts as a lane, becomes a track and then joins a metalled road. Motorists will need to go another mile or so to the signposted turning, on to a road which can be congested in the holiday season. The abbey was a twelfth-century Cistercian foundation in a typically remote spot. When building started the plan obviously allowed for enormous size. It would certainly have been the largest abbey in Wales and among the largest in Britain. The 242ft nave is exceeded only by those of York, Durham and Winchester cathedrals. It comes as a surprise, therefore, to find that this huge building was designed for about fifty monks. In fact it was never completed. The abbey's history was one of instability, as it found itself caught between the ambitions of the Welsh princes and the English kings. It suffered attacks from both sides, even when under the protection of the powerful Mortimer family; indeed it was finally destroyed by Owain Glyndwr in 1401 as part of his campaign against the Mortimers.

The abbey ruins also featured in another episode of history. During the Civil War they were fortified by Royalist sympathisers, only to be captured by Sir Thomas Middleton. After this the remains had a succession of private owners, and archaeological investigations in the early nineteenth century uncovered a great many relics. Little remains today (the tradition that the grave of Llewelyn ap Gruffydd, last of the native Princes of Wales, is located here is open to doubt) but six of the original nave arches were built into Llanidloes church when it was enlarged, and can be seen there today.

After the diversion to Abbey Cwmhir the road descends uneventfully to Crossgates and the junction with the Rhayader road. **Rhayader** cannot be claimed as part of the border country, but most visitors to this area will go through it sooner or later to reach the **Elan Valley** reservoir complex, highly commended as a tour. When the Corporation of Birmingham decided to buy the seventy square miles of the Elan and Claerwen valleys the plan was to build three reservoirs in each. The Elan scheme was completed and in use by 1904, but the plans for Claerwen were shelved until after the Second World War. Between 1946 and 1952 the Claerwen dam was added to the complex but plans for the other two dams were abandoned.

The proximity of the Elan Valley has done much to sustain the popularity of our next stopping place, **Llandrindod Wells**. After some deeply rural countryside it comes as a surprise to find a place that has all the attributes of a sophisticated spa town. Indeed, its wide streets, grand buildings, elegant terraces, lawns and parks are unique in the border country. Llandrindod (the name means the Church of the Trinity) has had a stop-start history, unlike many spas that found themselves famous almost overnight. This may be the reason for its resilience; certainly it has not retreated into the shabby gentility that has been the fate of other watering-places.

There is evidence of the local saline springs being used in the seventeenth

Radnor and the Central Welsh Border

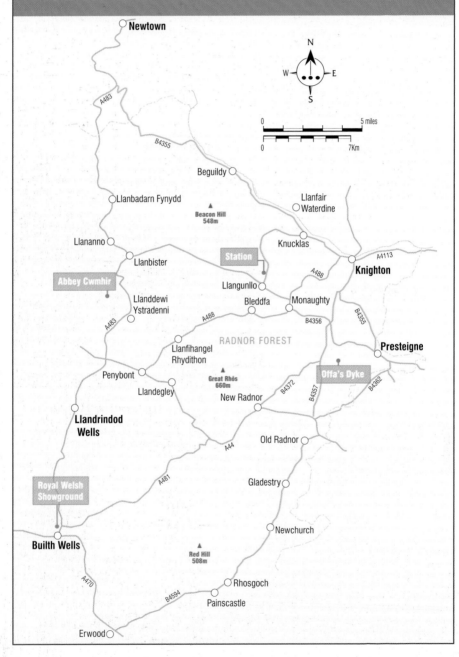

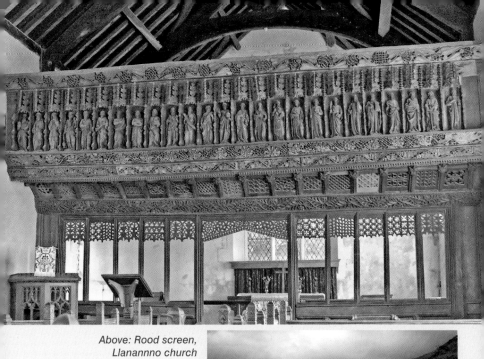

Above: Rood screen, Llanannno church

Right and below: The Elan Valley

century (the Romans probably appreciated them before that), but it was not until the middle of the eighteenth century that the waters were seriously exploited. In 1749, virtually at a stroke, a huge hotel was built overlooking the lake. It was designed as a fashionable social centre, and a rather incongruous one, being marooned in one of the least-populated areas of Britain. For a long time the hotel was the town, offering shops, sports and dances as well as highly-regarded standards of accommodation.

Unfortunately, the hotel also provided a suitably isolated venue for dubious weekends and discreditable gambling activities, and local opinion became firmly set against it. It closed in 1787, never having made serious use of the healing waters. It was the arrival of the railway in 1865 and the resurgence of the spa cult that gave the town a new lease of life. By the 1880s many thousands of visitors each year were coming to try the saline, sulphur, chalybeate and magnesium springs, and the status of Llandrindod had grown so rapidly that it became a meeting-place of the County Council. It is now the 'capital' of Powys and many of the County Council staff work in the old Pump House Hotel.

A walk around Llandrindod Wells

The waters have long since ceased to be a major attraction, and the town has developed as a centre for conferences and tourism. Nevertheless, its distinctive character justifies a short explora-

tion, for which the obvious starting point is the **Metropole Hotel**, one of the most imposing buildings. It is an Edwardian structure, and its central block is typically gabled. Enlargement and modernisation has been successfully unified by the elegant full-length verandah. This gives the hotel a recognisable 'spa' appearance, enhanced by the pleasant garden opposite.

Next door to the Metropole and flanking the Memorial Gardens are the **Town Hall and Museum**, with, between them, a nostalgic survival of former days – an ornamental grotto made from a peculiar substance called tufa. Moving up Temple Street and turning left you arrive at Middleton Street, a shopping centre which retains its own kind of dignity, being wide and free from heavy traffic. From the junction at the other end of Middleton Street two other notable hotels can be seen; the **Glen Usk** in South Crescent has some good ironwork, while the **Commodore** (formerly the rectory) is a splendid example of a Victorian urban mansion.

If you now go downhill and over the railway bridge there are some interesting arcaded shops in the demoted High Street, but dominating everything is the magnificent Victorian building of triangular design (formerly a hotel) now used as the District Council offices. To the left of this is Norton Terrace, which leads to one of Llandrindod's best-known features, the **Rock Park**.

The Park is a landscaped area of trees and paths with a stream running through, and at one end is the **Pump Room**, now restored to its former Betjemanesque eccentricity. In a dell in front of it, you can still find the tap providing free chalybeate water. Bowls enthusiasts will already be aware that Llandrindod is an international venue for the sport, and the extensive greens with fine hill views can be reached by walking up past the Pump Room.

The local authorities have done much to refurbish the old public meeting-places and social centres. In Ithon Road, running down the other side of the District Council offices, is the **Albert Hall**, a rather severe former chapel. It is now an attractive theatre, thanks to Council grants and the efforts of local volunteers. As you re-cross the railway and walk down Spa Road you pass the **Grand Pavilion**, which has also been given a face-lift in order to turn it into a conference centre. Close by is the church hall, a misleading term because, like many other things in Llandrindod, it is on the grand scale.

At the bottom of Spa Road is the town's main garage, and it seems entirely fitting that it should be called the Automobile Palace, a name redolent of old Daimlers and Lagondas. There is, in fact, **The National Cycle Collection** of rather less glamorous vintage bicycles here. It is worth going straight up the hill opposite to look at the former **Pump House Hotel**, a fine building on the site of one of the original springs. It is now the County Hall.

The road behind the Automobile Palace brings you to the **lake**, formed artificially in 1870 and perhaps a little overrated as a scenic feature. Somehow it never appears other than a grey expanse of featureless water, although there is compensation in the cheerful cafe serving good coffee. It is possible to walk round the lake, visiting on the way the original parish church, noted as the Place where the first Archbishop of the Church in Wales was formally elected in 1920. It was Llandrindod's parish church until dismissed as inadequate in the nineteenth century. In order to persuade the stubborn congregation to use the new Holy Trinity Church in town the roof of St Michael's was removed. This led to such an outcry that the church was restored in 1875 - an odd story of a very expensive mistake.

A leaflet from the Tourist Information Centre describes a good circular walk that takes in **Cefnllys**, a place of some interest because until 1885 it returned a Member of Parliament; in fact it was until then one of only six parliamentary boroughs in Radnorshire. It gained its status in Tudor times, and its administrative centre – the Court Leet – was at the nearby farmhouse of Neuadd. By 1832 the electorate of Cefnllys numbered about half a dozen and there were only three houses of any size. The walk also provides a chance to visit the Alpine Bridge, where the gorge is noted for its bird and plant life. Other recommended walks take you to the nearby villages of Disserth and Newbridge. Disserth church is well worth a visit because it has remained largely unchanged since the seventeenth century, with its box pews and three-decker pulpit, while Newbridge is a notable angling centre.

The next major stopping-place is **Builth Wells**. Its name indicates that it once had pretensions to spa status, but, unlike its neighbour, it failed to catch on, so there are few signs of grandeur here. There is not much frivolity either, although once a year the town comes

Above: National Cycle Collection, Llandrindod Wells

Above: The Glen Usk Hotel, Llandrindod Wells

Above: Royal Welsh Show, Builth Wells

to life when the **Royal Welsh Show** is held annually on its permanent site across the river.

The origins of the town lie in the fact that there was an important ford here, and a succession of castles has been sited on the high ground opposite the crossing-point. It was near here that Llewlyn ap Gruffydd, the last native Prince of Wales, was killed in 1282 after fleeing from Edward I's army in North Wales. Tradition has it that he was refused refuge in Builth Castle, and in addition to having this death on their consciences the townsfolk have encountered other major misfortunes. The Black Death was especially severe here, and in 1691 a disastrous fire destroyed virtually the whole town. An effort to promote Builth as a spa in the 1830s was a short-lived success, owing to

the poor access and the distance of the pump-room from the town. Since then the inhabitants seem to have made up their minds to live unobtrusively and not to tempt providence with any further imaginative enterprises.

Even the Wye can do little to enliven the scene. The fact that this was once a ford indicates that the river is normally placid here, and even in flood it merely takes on a sullen air, whereas a little further downstream it foams and leaps excitingly. The six-arched bridge constructed in 1779 and widened in 1925, stands precisely at a right-angled bend in the river. At its southern end is the market hall, easily the town's most attractive building, and, until recently, housing the Wyeside Arts Centre as well. The castle mound lies above the bridge but is on private ground and not normally accessible. **High Street**, with most of the shops and a pleasantly varied assortment of homely architecture, runs up from the bridge towards the church, which incorporates an odd conglomeration of styles, combining a massive fourteenth-century tower with a Victorian nave and chancel. The restorers failed to transfer much from the previous church, apart from an

43

effigy of John Lloyd, servant to Elizabeth I, which was placed, possibly as an afterthought, in the porch.

Builth has something of the atmosphere of a quarry town, and indeed the Llanelwedd quarries are visible from the bridge. Much of the stone for the Elan Valley reservoir construction came from here, and the hillsides are still worked today, though mainly for roadstone. The other main economic factor in the town's life is, of course, agriculture. It is reflected in the range of shops, and there is a lively cattle market on Mondays.

Before leaving Builth walkers should make sure they have the the local OS maps and as many walks leaflets as they can pick up at the tourist information centre at the car park, because the itinerary that follows provides some of the best walking opportunities in Britain.

Into remote Radnor

The direct route south from Builth is the A470, but you may prefer to pick up the B4567 at Llanelwedd and travel down the other side of the river in order to visit the famous **Aberedw Rocks** high above the river six miles below Builth. According to legend, Llewelyn ap Gruffydd came to Aberedw while being pursued by Edward I's men and hired a local blacksmith to reverse the shoes on his horse, so that the tracks he made would appear to be leading in the opposite direction. He spent the night in a cave among the Rocks (it can still be seen) but was betrayed by the blacksmith and had to flee. After his unsuccessful attempt to get refuge in Builth Castle, he and his men were killed close by. A large stone commemorating the event can be seen by the road at the neighbouring hamlet of Cilmery.

A short distance downstream there is a bridge which brings you to **Erwood**, on the western side of the river. For centuries there was a famous ford here, the favourite crossing-place for Welsh drovers on their way to England, and many hair-raising stories have survived of their efforts to get cattle across when the Wye was in flood. Erwood has another, unexpected, claim to fame. When the London writer Henry Mayhew was forced to escape his creditors for a while, he lodged here, and it was while he was having a quiet drink in the Erwood Inn that the idea of founding a humorous magazine occurred to him, and so Punch was born.

The old drover's road from Erwood is now the B4594. It starts at the bridge and is a good way to begin an exploration of the Radnor 'interior'. Almost as soon as you start, there is a desirable diversion. Two miles from Erwood a turn to the right takes you to the falls at **Craig Pwll Du**. About three miles further on at **Llanbach Howey** another lane to the south gives access to a whole jumble of tracks around the Begwns, the summit of which (at nearly 1400 feet) can be reached quite easily by following the Ordnance Survey map.

By this time the nature of this remarkably remote countryside becomes clear. To the right of the road there is a network of navigable lanes into the Wye Valley, but the area to the left is crossed only by tracks and paths. **Painscastle** is the first village of any size along the road. It was once an important town, fought over several times, and Henry III had his court here for a short time.

Nothing survives of the castle, although the defensive earthworks are still in evidence to the south of the village. A lane leading north from Painscastle is the starting-point for several long rambles in the hills. One possible objective is Red Hill, standing at 1600 feet. The best route is around the west side. A return can be made via Hondon and Llettypeod. A mile or so beyond **Rhosgoch**, the next village along from Painscastle, is a lane that brings you within walking distance of **Colva**, another challenging hill. Other routes abound on the map, but good equipment, including a compass, is advised. Rhosgoch Common, incidentally, is an expanse of a marsh of some interest to botanists.

Five miles further on from Rhosgoch is **Newchurch**, standing at the junction of three river valleys and one of the best bases for walking in the area, offering everything from a gentle stroll to a strenuous all-day ramble. The last major village on the B4594 is **Gladestry**, where there is access to Hergest Ridge, which forms the Welsh border here and provides further enjoyable walking.

At the point where the B4594 finally joins the A44 you can stop and admire the impressive **Stanner Rocks**. Turn left at the junction and then left again at Walton in order to reach **Old Radnor**. This tiny settlement is another example of an early village being abandoned in favour of a 'planned' town nearby. Old Radnor church, however, remains famous. It is in an elevated position (one of the few churches with a compelling view from its windows) and is full of treasures inside. The tub font attracts attention at once; it is pre-Norman and said to be the largest in Britain.

The wide rood screen is superb, but the unique feature of the church is the organ case of linen-fold panelling dating from the sixteenth century. You return to the main road and turn left for **New Radnor**, a large village with its church set up high among the trees and its roads still tracing out the early medieval ground plan. There is nothing left of its once formidable castle, but remains of the old town walls survive on the southern edge of the village.

Around the Radnor Forest

Here we are on the border of that convoluted mass of hills that make up the **Radnor Forest**. Roads run all round it, but any exploration of the Forest itself must be on foot. Local leaflets provide information about the walking possibilities, but it is worth mentioning a short walk to the famous falls known as **Water-break-its-neck**. You leave the A44 two miles south-west of New Radnor and follow the lane into the Warren plantation. The falls are about eighty feet high and fall into a dark ravine, but don't expect anything spectacular during a dry spell.

Continue on the A44 from New Radnor to reach **Llandegley**. It is an interesting village for two reasons. First, it was a miniature spa, with saline, sulphur and chalybeate springs that, in the middle ages, attracted pilgrims suffering from a type of epilepsy called St Tegla's disease. The **Well House** can still be seen in a field near the village centre. Its other notable feature is the isolated Quaker meeting-house known as **The Pales**, a mile or so to the north. The site, commanding magnificent views, was first established in 1673, and the permanent meeting house was built in 1717. Quaker activity has fluctuated since, but in the late 1970s the graveyard was restored, the cottage renovated and the meeting house itself re-thatched. It is now used for religious conferences and similar functions. From the churchyard at Llandegley there is a good walk up to the **Llandegley Rocks**.

The route round the Radnor Forest continues with a right turn on to the A488 at **Penybont**. **Llanfihangel Rhydithon**, three miles further on. This village looks over the Aran valley and has its back to some of the wildest country in Radnor. It is the access point for a notable track that crosses the Forest range completely and finishes at Water-break-its-neck. The A488 passes through remote countryside to reach **Bleddfa**, literally 'The Place of the Wolves' and a sufficient indication of its former remoteness. (Apparently the last wolf in the Radnor Forest was killed here in the sixteenth century.) Like many other settlements Bleddfa suffered at the hands of Owain Glyndwr, whose men burned the church tower in 1401, and this incident was vividly substantiated when excavation in the late 1960s revealed the blackened remains of the tower. They can now be seen next to the church. An interesting feature of the interior is the roof, which retains some of the original painted colouring on its timbers. The church is now in the care of a local Trust, whose members aim to restore it fully, not only as a place of worship but as a cultural centre. A lane north-west from Bleddfa through Dolaney Farm leads to the attractive St Michael's Pool. The walk can be extended by taking another lane northeast from the Pool to the village of **Llangunllo**, standing near the source of the river Lugg in an impressive situation, surrounded by hills.

From Bleddfa the A488 moves on to cross the Lugg and to reach a junction with the B4356. At this point you are bound to notice the large, rather gaunt house standing by the road. It is Elizabethan, and its name – Monaughty – looks Irish, but in fact it is a corruption of the Welsh 'Mynach-dy', 'The Place of the Monk'. The explanation is that when Abbey Cwmhir was dissolved, the Abbot retired to one of the monastic community's farms, the site of which lies beside the river a mile towards Llangunllo.

Having turned on to the B4356, you pass, within a mile, the site of the battle of **Pilleth**, when Owain Glyndwr defeated and slaughtered an English army composed mainly of Herefordshire men under Sir Edmund Mortimer. The battle is referred to with grisly implications at the beginning of Shakespeare's Henry IV, Part One. Pilleth had become famous before this as a place of pilgrimage for people hoping to be relieved by the waters of a nearby well, said to be particularly effective for eye disease. The church, virtually rebuilt in the 1890s, stands isolated above the battlefield, and from this direction you will need to watch carefully for the entrance through Pilleth Court. There is a circular walk starting and finishing at Pilleth Court and encircling Graig Hill.

There is now no reason to stop before **Presteigne**, a placid town right on the

Right: New Radnor Church

Below: A magnificent section of Offa's Dyke. Its approximate position is marked on the map on p.38

border (in fact on the 'wrong' side of Offa's Dyke). Despite this, it was formerly the county town of Radnorshire, and some of its buildings reflect this former importance. The most striking is undoubtedly the **Radnorshire Arms**, a seventeenth-century black and white inn whose unusually large and inviting porch has protruding steps. **The Duke's Arms**, boasting a galleried yard, rivals it in interest. Another of Presteigne's gems is the early nineteenth-century **Shire Hall** (now the Judge's Lodging), an elegant building in a vaguely classical style but fitting well into the proportions of the town. The building has been transformed into an entertaining inter active museum that features not only the judge's rooms but the servants' quarters. **St Andrew's Church** is, by general consent, the finest medieval church in Radnor. While still used for worship it also hosts regular exhibitions by noted artists, but its greatest treasure is the Presteigne Tapestry, Flemish in origin and woven in the early sixteenth century. The tapestry, depicting Christ's entry into Jerusalem, has recently been the subject of conservation.. The rest of the town centre is mainly in a quiet Georgian style, providing an air of restful solidity.

The B4355 north from Presteigne is the road to Knighton. On the way you pass through the large and attractive village of **Norton**, which, as the name implies, was a Saxon settlement. The church, which by all accounts was rather run down in the early nineteenth century, is a good example of sympathetic restoration by the distinguished architect Sir Giles Gilbert Scott. He rebuilt the bell turret in the original style and restored the fine rood screen, using much of the original carving. The enlightened squire who had the work done in 1868 was Sir Richard Green-Price, who was also responsible for bringing rail communications to Radnorshire. It was Sir Richard who planted a grove of trees on the spot where a large number of human bones were disinterred near Pilleth and presumed to be those of the English soldiers killed in the battle.

And so to **Knighton**, which has some claim to be the border town, since it is right on **Offa's Dyke** and has some of the finest stretches of the long-distance path on the hills to either side. Not surprisingly it is the headquarters of the Offa's Dyke Association, and your first visit should be to their centre, where you can obtain a wealth of information and inexpensive literature about the Dyke, its path and various other walks in the district. Knighton itself an attractive place, with hilly streets and pleasant buildings, best seen in the picturesque thoroughfares of The Narrows, a series of streets where the buildings are of the seventeenth century or older. An unusual attraction is the Powys Observatory, home to a powerful astronomical telescope and also offering a planetarium show. The surrounding countryside can be observed through a camera obscura.

The final section of this tour is to the north-west of Knighton up the **Teme valley**. The route is the B4355, and the first village is **Knucklas**, which boasts an unexpectedly grandiose railway viaduct. It is a tiny place now, but resembles Cefnllys in having been a fully-fledged borough represented in Parliament until 1885. Its near neighbour on the road,

Llanfair Waterdine, has a particularly fine length of Offa's Dyke above it, accessible by way of a lane north of the village. Equally worthwhile is the walk to Beacon Hill to the west of the road. At 2000 feet, this is one of the highest points in the Radnor area. Beguildy is spelt thus on the map, but originally it was Bugeildy, 'The Shepherd's House'. It is a final reminder of the contribution that the Radnor, Clun and Kerry Forests have made to sheep farming, including the introduction of two distinct breeds. Beguildy church is yet another that was remote enough to escape the 'reformers' and consequently retained its intricate fourteenth-century rood screen.

Between Beguildy and Felindre, there are a multitude of paths and tracks leading into the hills to the south. After Felindre the road, which has hitherto been fairly level, starts to climb steeply up to Kerry Hill, providing final spectacular views over the Clun Forest. The last part of the journey is a gradual winding descent into Newtown.

The area south of Radnor is covered in chapter 3.

Places to Visit

Llandrindod Wells

Tourist information

Automobile Palace, Princes Ave, Llandrindod Wells.
☎ 01597 822600
Groe Street car park, Builth Wells
☎ 01982 553307

Rock Park

Pleasant park housing the picturesque and fully-restored Rock Spa Pump Room and Pavilion. Town centre.

National Cycle Collection

The Automobile Palace, Temple Street, Llandrindod Wells.
☎ 01597 825531
England's principal museum of cycles and cycling housed in splendid garage of 1910.

Radnorshire Museum

Temple Steet, Llandrindod Wells
☎ 01597 824513
Very comprehensive museum of local history and social life.

Albert Hall

Ithon Street, Llandrindod Wells
☎ 01597 822324
Arts and performance centre

Abbey Cymhir

6 miles north of Llandrindod Wells, off A483.
Important site of major medieval abbey.

The Hall at Abbey Cym-hir

☎ 01597 851727
Tours of 52-room house in Gothic Revival style, breathtakingly furnished. Extensive gardens.

Places to Visit

Royal Welsh Showground

At Llanelwedd, 10 miles south of Llandrindod Wells.
☎ 01982 554406
Royal Welsh Show in July. Events throughout the year.

Elan Valley Reservoirs

Complex of reservoirs supplying Birmingham. Impressive dams, fine scenery.
15 miles west of Llandrindod, via A4081/A470.

Radnor Forest

Tourist Information

Judge's Lodging, Presteigne
☎ 01544 260650

Offa's Dyke Centre

West Street, Knighton
☎ 01547 528753
Devoted to Offa'a Dyke and its long-distance footpath. Also general tourist information.

Old Radnor Church

Off A44 at Walton, 7 miles south-west of Presteigne.
Church of exceptional interest. Huge pre-Norman font.

Ralphs Cider & Perry

Old Badland Farm, New Radnor LD8 2TG
☎ 01544 350304
National Goldmedal winner. Ring ahead if visiting.

The Pales

1 mile north of Llandegley.
Very early Quaker meeting house, impressively situated.

St Andrew's Church, Presteigne

Finest medieval church in Radnor. Also hosts art exhibitions and houses famous Presteigne Tapestry of early sixteenth century.

The Judge's Lodging

Broad Street, Presteigne
☎ 01544 260650
Open: 1st Mar–31st Oct, daily 10am-5pm, 1st Nov–22nd Dec Wed-Sun 10am-4pm. Closed Jan & Feb.
Former Shirehall, now reconstructed in its original form as courtroom and judge's quarters.

Withybeds Nature Park

Beside River Lugg on eastern outskirts of Presteigne Marshland habitat supporting varied plant and bird life.

Whimble Nursery/Gardens

Kinnerton, LD8 2PD
NE of Rhayader, brown signs from Walton (A44)
☎ 01547 560413
Open: Easter–mid-Oct, Thu-Sun, BH Mon 10.30am-5.30pm

3. The Lower Wye Valley and the Forest of Dean

Tintern Abbey

Chapter 1 took us as far as Hereford, and we now begin an exploration of the border countryside to the south, including the fascinating Forest of Dean.

The Lower Wye and the Forest of Dean

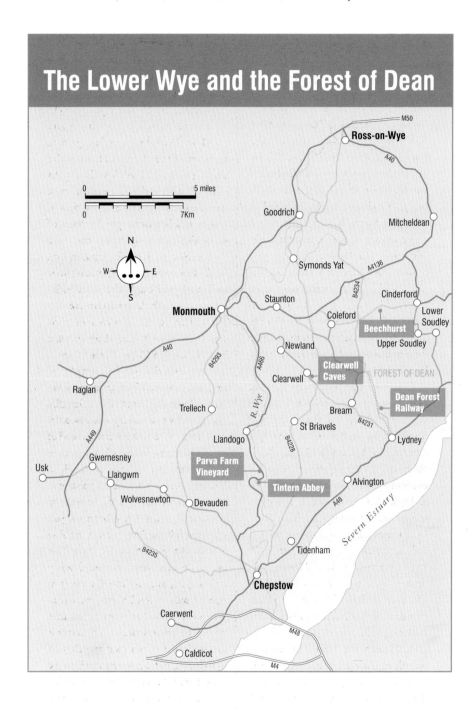

Ross and Monmouth

Our exploration of this southernmost border area begins in **Ross-on-Wye**. The Wye loops sharply here, and the best view of Ross is from the river bank below the town, from which pleasant buildings rise in terraces towards St Mary's church with its elegant spire. The dominant figure whose name recurs in the history of Ross was John Kyrle, celebrated as the 'Man of Ross' in some of Alexander Pope's less inspired verse. He was obviously a remarkable man. Much of the town's present layout is his work, and in the course of his 87 years from 1637 to 1724 he was responsible for countless charitable acts that endeared him to the local population.

The seventeenth-century **Market Hall**, an unassuming sandstone building, stands at the head of the bustling Broad Street. On its north wall is a carving of a heart and the letters FC, signifying 'faithful to Charles in heart', a device expressing Kyrle's intense monarchism and placed there so that he could see it from his house opposite. The house itself is now divided into a shop and offices, and in the garden behind is Kyrle's summerhouse. Oddly enough, no memorial was erected to Kyrle until fifty years after his death, when a large monument was placed in the sanctuary of the church.

St Mary's is a light and spacious building, dating basically from the thirteenth century, and a good deal of the glass in the east window is original. There are some notable memorials here apart from Kyrle's, including the one to the Rudhall family, who were also benefactors of the town. The churchyard contains an interesting cross commemorating over 300 victims of an epidemic of the plague in 1637 who were buried in a nearby plague pit. **The Prospect**, a public garden, lies west of the churchyard and is the starting point of Kyrle's Walk, a path which he supplied with trees and seats. These seem to have been the victims of early vandalism, or simply the desire of successive parish priests for firewood. The centre of Ross is harmonious, with few outstanding individual buildings, although the sixteenth-century **Rudhall Almshouses** in Church Street are worth seeing, as are the **Webbe's Almshouses** of a century later in Copse Cross Street.

Probably the first example of organised tourism in England was the cruise down the lower Wye, a lengthy excursion that proved especially popular with poets and artists towards the end of the eighteenth century, when the craze for 'romantic' scenery was at its height. Unfortunately it is no longer possible to take a boat the full distance. To start the journey down the Wye Valley today you take the A40 for Monmouth, crossing Wilton Bridge just outside Ross. This riverside area has been pleasantly landscaped, and Wilton Castle (not open) stands nearby. The busy main road follows the Wye for about four miles, when the river swings away towards **Goodrich**. A minor road branches off to follow it, and this brings you into the village past 'Ye Hostelrie', a pub that is in fact a turreted folly. Since there is no parking space in Goodrich you will need to pay to get into the picnic

Goodrich Castle

Canoeing on the River Wye at Ross-on-Wye

Above: Amazing Maze with creators Lindsey and Edward Heyes

Left: Monnow Bridge, Monmouth

International Centre for Birds of Prey

Lots to see and do including; flying demonstrations; book shop; coffee shop serving home cooked food; aviaries housing a diverse collection of raptors as well as variety of courses on offer.

Contact
The International Centre for Birds of Prey
Boulsdon House, Newent,
Gloucestershire, GL18 1JJ
Tel: 01531 820286 or 01531 821581
email: jpj@icbp.org www.icbp.org

site next to the **castle.** This is a most impressive ruin in sandstone, rising from solid rock. The twelfth-century keep is the oldest portion, while the remainder is at least a century newer. One of the more interesting features inside is the small chapel that once had a rood loft. The castle remained virtually intact until the Civil War, when it was ruined by Parliamentary siege forces.

If you leave Goodrich by the B4229 you will arrive after half a mile at a narrow road signposted **Symonds Yat.** It is one of the routes to a very old and famous viewpoint, crossing the river and passing over a flat expanse with Coppet Hill to the left, Huntsham Hill in front and, over to the right, the scattered hillside dwellings of Great Doward. Continue uphill when the road forks until you reach the Forestry Commission car park. The Yat Rock is a few hundred yards away. As a tourist attraction it may be hackneyed but the view from the rock is none the less remarkable. Down below there appear to be two parallel rivers. They are, of course, both the Wye, and what you see are the beginning and end of a huge loop concealed from view by Huntsham Hill.

After re-joining the A40 there is little to stop for before **Monmouth,** which deserves a long stay. It is worth noting that parking is not easy, and it is advisable to make for the first car park you see signposted.

Coming from Ross you enter the town from the 'wrong' end, and the thing to do is to walk immediately down Monnow Street to the one surviving thirteenth-century gatehouse incorporated into the **Monnow Bridge,** an almost unique defensive feature last pressed into service during the Chartist unrest of the early nineteenth century. The small arches on each side were made to accommodate pavements when the road was widened in the nineteenth century. The suburb of **Over Monnow** has its own attractions, one of them being the church of St Thomas next to the bridge, originally Norman and heavily restored, but still boasting a superb original chancel arch.

A leisurely walk back along Monnow Street will reveal a pleasant mixture of unpretentious architecture with the best buildings on the right hand side, in particular the Robin Hood Inn, Chippenham House and Cornwall House. At the top of the street the buildings of the old town centre close in tightly, squashed as they are by the bottleneck formed by the Wye on one side and its tributary the Monnow on the other.

Agincourt Square is the heart of the town, dominated by the eighteenth-century Shire Hall, the site of the street market. The name of the square is a reminder that Henry V was born in the castle here in 1387, and a rather coy statue of him occupies a niche on the front of the Hall. Monmouth's other famous local boy, Charles Rolls, is remembered in more robust fashion by a statue at ground level, showing the motoring and aviation pioneer studying a model plane with some satisfaction. The Shire Hall is flanked by two fine old pubs, the King's Head and the Beaufort Arms.

Behind the square to the west are the ruins of the castle and also the magnificent **Great Castle House.** Only the remnants of the Great Tower and the Great Hall are visible on the castle site, and the seventeenth-century house is much more interesting. Unfortunately they can only be visited by special arrangement. The curving Priory Street contains the Market Hall, a classical building dating from the 1830s but rebuilt in the 1960s after a fire. It now houses a local history centre and also the Nelson Museum, originally based on a collection of Nelson memorabilia donated to the town by the mother of Charles Rolls but now covering a much wider scope. The **church of St Mary** is not particularly distinguished, being a nineteenth-century reconstruction of an eighteenth-century reconstruction, and its most graceful feature is probably the slender spire. This part of the town repays a close inspection of its handsome, small-scale architecture.

The by-pass may have made the town more pleasant to walk in, but it has also ruined the frontage to the Wye, because the massive embankment of the A40 effectively seals Monmouth off from the river. However, the road does not succeed in dominating the Gothic architecture of **Monmouth School** opposite the bridge by which you leave to resume the drive down the Wye.

Through the Lower Wye Valley to Chepstow

The road out of Monmouth is the A466, which at this point runs along the fringe of the Forest of Dean, passing first through Redbrook, where there is little to see now, although it was once an important industrial settlement. After Redbrook you drive along a fine wooded valley before crossing the river at the elegant **Bigsweir** bridge, a convenient point of access to the path that runs along the left bank. On the Welsh side of the bridge a minor road turns off to Whitebrook, noted for its papermills, some of which can still be seen converted into houses. Opposite this turning is the site of a riverside railway station, a relic of the Wye Valley line that followed the river closely.

At **Llandogo**, a mile further on, you may well be put off by the commercialised road frontage, but it is in fact a village with a fascinating history as the upper limit of tidal navigation. It was here that the cargoes of boats that had sailed from Chepstow were transferred to shallow-draught barges hauled by large teams of men. Several of the gravestones in the churchyard are adorned with anchors and there is still a nautical air about the place. There is access from the village to various viewpoints and picnic sites in the woods above.

Two miles from Llandogo there is a lay-by on the right, your only chance to park in order to visit the riverside settlement of **Brockweir** on the other bank. It is a picturesque place now with its wharves, old houses and Moravian chapel, and it is hard to believe that it once ranked next to Chepstow as a Wye port and was noted for its shipbuilding. The river trade declined with the coming of the railway and Brockweir is now a quiet residential village. A few hundred yards after Brockweir look out for a lane to the left leading

Above: Chepstow Castle and (right) Chepstow from the air
Cadw, Welsh Assembly Government (Crown Copyright)

to the former **Tintern station.** The station has been imaginatively restored, complete with station building, signal box, signals, length of track and a coach. The signal box houses a useful information centre and refreshments are available in a waiting-room full of railway memorabilia.

After this it is only a short distance to the valley's most famous attraction, though much of the magic of **Tintern Abbey** has been dissipated by the garishness of the adjacent village and the commercialism of the site itself. However, if you turn your back on the cafe and gift shop it is still possible to appreciate the splendid ruins, especially from inside the ruined nave. The first Abbey was built here in 1131, but the present building dates from the late thirteenth century and is still in a remarkable state of preservation. After the dissolution of the monasteries a metal works was set up on the site, and a plaque on the wall records the fact that brass was first successfully made here.

The road now begins to climb steadily, and at the point where it emerges from the woodland at the top there is a minor road on the right leading to the **Wynd Cliff**, a celebrated viewpoint. The area is now managed by Forestry Enterprises which has set up a picnic site and nature trail, but the most famous feature here is the steep path, created in 1829, known as the 365 steps.

The big racecourse on the left indicates that you are approaching **Chepstow.** It is a town with a long history as a port and ship-building centre, and although little evidence of it remains today the most interesting part of the town is still the area that lies within the loop of the Wye. From the Town Gate the handsome and cheerful High Street slopes down to **Beaufort Square**, from which narrower thoroughfares lead down to the river. The Square is the natural focal point of the town, and there is space to sit and decide which way to go next.

To the east Station Road leads to the former shipyard area and a fine converted flour mill. The cobbled Hocker Hill Street has some of the most picturesque buildings, including the eighteenth-century Powis Almshouses, while St Mary Street is a mellow blend of old and new shop fronts with interesting upper storeys. The two latter roads both take you to Church Street, which has the very large parish church at its east end. It has to be said that the **church**, fairly ruthlessly altered in the nineteenth century, has little to distinguish it apart from a decorated Norman doorway left in the eighteenth-century tower. By going down Lower Church Street you reach **The Back,** the riverside area that was the centre of Chepstow's commercial life as a port. The steep limestone cliffs opposite catch the eye, as does the railway bridge. Brunel built the original in 1852 as a suspension bridge, and although a new central span was installed in the 1960s his bold iron columns remain. The superb iron road bridge has survived much longer, having been built in 1816.

The castle comes into view here, sprawling alongside the river on its long, narrow site. It is a huge structure, and the earliest section, the Great Tower, is unusual in having been constructed in stone in very early Norman times. The castle was progessively enlarged and strengthened, although the defences were not really tested until the Civil War,

when the Parliamentarians besieged and eventually captured it. No extensive damage resulted and it was inhabited until fairly recently. You reach the entrance by walking up Bridge Street. The small **Chepstow Museum** is immediately opposite the castle gate, and Bridge Street itself boasts a fine terrace of early nineteenth-century houses.

It is not often that a town itinerary includes the main car park, but Chepstow's is rather different. Not only is it a good vantage point for a striking close-up view of the castle but it is bounded by a stretch of the thirteenth-century **Portwall**, which originally sealed off the town on the landward side. It connects with the Town Gate and continues even more impressively on the other side, running past the 'garden suburb' of **Hardwick**, an interesting early experiment in the use of concrete for housebuilding.

The area to the south-west, now

Above: Usk

effectively cut off by the M4, is low-lying and fairly nondescript in character, but there are three places of interest in the Newport direction that can be visited in the course of an afternoon.

On to Usk

By leaving Chepstow on the A48, crossing the motorway and turning left on to the B4245 you can get to **Caldicot.** It is a dull town in itself, but tucked away behind the housing estates is the castle, originally twelfth-century and restored with some skill in the nineteenth. The buildings are extensive and the gatehouse is especially impressive. Regular medieval banquets are held in the hall above it. The surrounding park is freely accessible.

Caerwent, to the north of Caldicot, was the Roman town of Venta Silurum, and its present buildings sit casually among some remarkable remains. The most obvious feature is the extensive wall, over 15ft high in places, but right next to the main street are the foundations of a temple. Continue west along the A48 and you arrive at **Penhow,** where the castle (inhabited and rather different from the others in the neighbourhood) is now a major tourist attraction, with elaborate visual and auditory aids for the visitor.

To the north-west of Chepstow the country is high, clear and invigorating, and although the Usk lacks the drama of the Wye it has been far less commercialised. The way out is the B4235, which after five miles passes the **Wentwood Forest** to the left. There

are the usual picnic sites and forest trails here, with the additional attraction of the Wentwood Reservoir where fishing is possible. At Llangwm a right turn leads to **Wolvesnewton,** where the model farm and folk collection are likely to be of special interest to children. There is a craft centre and a programme of temporary exhibitions during the summer. If you take the left turn in Llangwm you will reach the **Gwent Ski Centre,** which sounds unlikely until you realise that the skiing is on grass. All the necessary equipment can be hired.

A few hundred yards beyond this crossroads is an inconspicuous right turn at the top of the hill. It leads to **Llangwm's two churches.** The first, St John's, is small, simple and unremarkable, but St Jerome's, a short distance further along the lane, is surprisingly large, with a magnificent tower and the finest rood screen in the area. Equally attractive is the little church at **Gwernesney,** situated just before the point where the B4235 crosses the A449.

Usk is smaller than you might expect. Best known for its fishing and its agricultural college, it does not go out of its way to attract tourists, although the **Rural Life Museum** in Newmarket Street makes an interesting stop. The church, too, should be visited – it has a famous and splendid organ, bought from Llandaff Cathedral in 1899. The castle is privately owned, but the ruins of the **Priory** are freely accessible next to the church. On the far side of the bridge carrying the Pontypool road is the picnic site known as **The Island,** and a locally-produced pamphlet details several walks from it. The left turn on the other side of this bridge (signposted Llanbadoc) leads to the **Llandegfedd Reservoir**, where boats can be hired and where there is a farm park with rare breeds, vintage machinery and an adventure playground.

There is a direct road from Usk to and its famous castle. Having been built in the fifteenth century (unusually late) **Raglan Castle** is a sophisticated structure, designed to resist cannon balls rather than arrows. The Great Tower is a castle within a castle, having its own moat and planned as a final place of refuge. In fact the castle developed into a comfortable residence, and the most serious action there was in 1646 when it was captured by Parliamentary forces and systematically ruined. There is still a great deal to see and a visit is highly recommended.

The scenic route back to Chepstow is the B4293, a turning off the A40 just before Monmouth. Five miles along it is **Trelleck**, once a very important town and therefore possessing an unusually large church. A very old preaching cross is prominent in the churchyard, and inside there is a curious seventeenth-century sundial showing Trelleck's three tourist attractions – the Harold Stones (origin unknown) that stand in a field on the left of the B4293 to the south of the village, a Norman motte called The Tump in a farmyard to the south-west of the church, and the Virtuous Well (probably an early spa) just outside the village on the left of the minor road to Tintern.

Exploring the Forest of Dean

The 200 square miles of the Forest of Dean were originally designated as a royal hunting ground, certainly from Norman times and possibly earlier. As such it acquired its own laws and privileges, including its Court of Verderers, charged with the care of the Forest and still doing so today. Protected by the rivers Severn and Wye, the Forest gained a distinctive, rather introverted character, with a population fiercely protective of its way of life and discouraging outsiders. This has been evident in its long history of coal mining, which could only be done by 'Free Miners' – local men who had duly qualified for the privilege. Fortunately the residents are much more open to visitors today, and the Forest has become a favourite destination for those who appreciate its fine woodland and unique industrial heritage .

The Forest is an intricate area with tremendous scope for the walker. As a Forest Park it has been sympathetically developed for recreation, and its well-charted paths provide a whole range of expeditions, from short family rambles to more serious long-distance walks. It would be superfluous to detail the walks in this chapter since the guides produced by the Forestry Commission and other bodies are readily available locally. You may also be able to pick up H.W. Paar's pamphlet *An industrial tour of the Wye Valley and the Forest of Dean*, which provides a clear guide to the wealth of old industrial sites and relics

Raglan Castle

in the Forest. Since the long-stay visitor is so well provided with literature, the rest of this chapter is designed for those with limited time who want to sample the Forest's unique atmosphere.

Monmouth is a suitable starting point, and the way out is the A4136. Very soon after crossing the river and branching left you need to look out for a concealed right turn that will take you up to the **Kymin**. This is a famous viewpoint, but it has an odd additional feature – the 'Naval Temple', bearing the names of sixteen British admirals. If you miss the turn to the Kymin you can stop at a parking place on the right a mile and a half further on and walk up to the **Buckstone**, which commands an equally fine view.

Staunton is the first village along this road, and its wind-swept church is well worth a visit. Among other features is a pulpit with a staircase leading from it up to a former rood loft, and its sanctuary is detached from the rest of the church by the central tower and the bell-ringing area beneath. Shortly after the village take right fork to **Coleford**, one of the small, functional towns characteristic of the Forest. There is nothing obviously picturesque here, unless it is the sight of an isolated church tower dividing the traffic in the town centre, but the Angel Hotel is a striking coaching inn.

Coleford is a convenient centre for some short expeditions. If you leave the town on the B4226 you quickly arrive at the **Hopewell Colliery Mining Museum,** and two miles further on is the famous **Speech House,** built in 1676 as a courthouse for the Foresters of Dean. It was known as the Court of Verderers, and it still meets theoretically every forty days, although in practice the four Verderers hold business meetings quarterly to carry out their duties, less concerned now with justice than with the safeguarding of the environment. Several forest trails begin at or near the Speech House.

North of the town the B4432 is an

alternative route to Symonds Yat, and the woodland on the western side of the road contains another network of forest trails. To the south there are two notable attractions that can be reached by taking the B4428 (St Briavels) road and branching right after less than two miles at the Lambsquay Hotel. The **Clearwell Caves,** a short way along this road, are in fact a group of eight caverns, part of a network of former iron mines. It is possible to go underground to see the workings, and there are also displays of machinery and equipment. The visit to Clearwell can be rounded

off by travelling the 2m north-west to **Newland**. Newland church is known as 'The Cathedral of the Forest', a title earned not so much by its size as by its open interior, which gives the effect of great spaciousness. The resemblance to a cathedral is reinforced by the number of memorials and small chapels. A useful guidebook, available in the church, details the many unusual features, the most famous of which is the 'Miner's Brass' in the Greyndour Chapel. It is believed to be the family crest and shows in remarkable detail the figure of a medieval forest miner with

Above and inset: Clearwell Caves

a hod and pick and holding a candle in his mouth. The attractive William Jones almshouses by the side of the church have superb stone tile roofs.

From Coleford we move south to **St Briavels**, a quiet village in an impressive position high above the Wye. The church is interesting, but more unexpected is the thirteenth-century castle, part of which now serves as a youth hostel. The two round gatehouse towers catch the eye, but there are residential buildings behind and the remains of a large moat. In its time it has been a courthouse and prison, but there is no record of any military action here. An unusual church is the main attraction at **Hewelsfield**, two miles to the south. The nave dates from Saxon times and the Normans added a squat tower. The chancel was added still later, and the result, as at Staunton, was to distance the sanctuary from the congregation. The exterior is dominated by the sweep of the nave roof, which extends almost to the ground.

So far the B4228 has not been of great interest, but it now starts to pass through high woodland with occasional glimpses of the Severn estuary. In fact there is a picnic site and viewpoint about two miles after Hewelsfield, and three miles further on is the famous **Wintour's Leap**. There is no official parking place here and you can easily miss it, so it is worth stopping where you can and walking to see this 200ft precipice, supposedly jumped on horseback by Sir John Wintour in 1642 when escaping from the Parliamentarians.

To avoid arriving back in Chepstow you need to take either the lane just before the Leap or the one after down towards the estuary to **Tidenham**. The church here has a Norman lead font and is also of interest because its tower once served as a navigation beacon for shipping. The lane through Tidenham meets the A48, and you turn left and start to travel parallel to the estuary shore towards Lydney. This is a dull road, and there are few good reasons for leaving it, unless it is to visit the interesting churches at **Woolaston** and **Alvington**, both very close to the road.

The last village before Lydney is **Aylburton**, which is dominated by **Lydney Park.** The gardens are occasionally open, especially in April and May when the rhododendrons and azaleas make a stunning show. In addition the Park contains the site of a Roman temple, with a museum of excavated objects, and the Forest Model Village, a great attraction for children.

Lydney is a busy modern town, and a major attraction lies a mile to the north on the B4234. It is the **Norchard Steam Centre**, run by the Dean Forest Railway members, who generously open their yard and allow enthusiasts to roam freely round their remarkable collection of locomotives and rolling stock in various stages of restoration. A standard gauge steam and diesel railway operates regular services between Lydney Junction and Norchard. **Bream,** three miles north-west of Lydney, is famous for its Roman iron workings known as The Scowles. They lie within woodland on the left just before you enter the village, and a public path starts in the village itself.

The A48 now runs direct to **Blakeney**, but a more attractive route is the B4234 past the Steam Centre, branching on to the B4431 at **Parkend,** a community rich in industrial history, which is covered in local leaflets. Three miles after Parkend a section of Roman road has been uncovered at **Blackpool Bridge.**

On reaching Blakeney you turn north again almost at once on the B4227 to pass through the spectacular **Soudley Valley,** which can be appreciated even by those not interested in industrial history. The **Dean Heritage Museum** by the road on the northern outskirts of Lower Soudley is dedicated to the history and traditions of the forest, and its central feature is an old watermill.

The long sprawl of Ruspidge merges imperceptibly into **Cinderford,** now a country town but once a centre of the mining industry. It has the utilitarian look of most Forest towns, although in recent years it has been developed for both commerce and leisure. A notable modern feature is Linear Park, an area to the west of the town, which has been landscaped with lakes and footpaths. The surrounding countryside is not without interest. At **Littledean,** on the A4151 to the east, is Dean Hall, a building that is claimed to span over 800 years of architectural history. Roman and Saxon traces have been found, and excavation is still going on. Quite apart from the interest of the building the grounds are extremely attractive. From here it is only a short distance to **Newnham,**

a pleasant place right on the edge of the Servern and with a church commanding a fine view across the river. One of the best buildings here is the seventeenth-century inn opposite the church.

Moving north from Cinderford on the A4151 you reach the crossroads at Nailbridge and make for Mitcheldean. The old spoilheaps in the field below Harrow Hill Church are very noticeable from the crossroads and typical of the area. In spite of the usual spread of modern housing **Mitcheldean** retains a good deal of character, with some half-timbered houses and a huge church with exceptionally fine roofs. A wooden screen between nave and chancel contains Tudor paintings of the Last Judgement, while the immense reredos has life-size marble figures.

While in Mitcheldean do not overlook the church at **Abenhall** (or Abinghall). This is a very old coalmining centre reached by way of a minor road south from the centre of Mitcheldean. The main treasure of the isolated church is a fifteenth-century octagonal font, presented by the Free Smiths and Guild of Miners and bearing their arms.

As a final memory of the Forest you might like to climb the 1000ft **May Hill** to the north-west of Mitcheldean. The simplest way to reach it is to follow the A4136, turn left at the junction with the A40 and into the village of Dursley Cross. A minor road from here brings you to the public footpath to the summit, which has extensive views to the south.

The A40 is the direct route back to Monmouth.

Places to Visit

Ross and Monmouth

Tourist Information

Edde Cross Street, Ross
☎ 01989 562768

Shire Hall, Monmouth

☎ 01600 713899

Cowdy Gallery

Contemporary Art Centre.
31 Culver Street, Newent, 10 miles
east of Ross.
☎ 01531 821173

International Centre for Birds of Prey

At Newent, 10 miles east of Ross.
☎ 01531 820286
160 birds of prey with daily flying
demonstrations. Pets corner for
children.

Newent Lake Park

In Newent, 10 miles east of Ross.
Originally part of private estate,
large and picturesque lake.

Three Choirs Vineyard

On B4215, 2 miles from Newent.
☎ 01531 890223

Violette Szabo Museum

At Wormelow, off A49, 8 miles
north-west of Ross.
☎ 01981 540477
Open: Apr–Oct, Wed 11am-1pm &
2pm-4pm
Commemorating life and
achievements of famous
Resistance heroine.

Goodrich Castle (English Heritage)

Off A40, 5 miles south of Ross.
☎ 01600 890538
Majestic castle ruins on red
sandstone crag.

Nelson Museum & Local History Centre, Monmouth

New Market Hall, Priory Street.
☎ 01600 710630
Wide range of displays illustrating
local history and social life, plus
Nelson memorabilia.
Off A40, 5 miles north-east of
Monmouth. HR9 6DA
Open: from 11am daily
Historic viewpoint, with panoramic
views over big loop in the river Wye.

Kingfisher Cruises

Symonds Yat East, off A40, 5 miles
north-east of Monmouth.
☎ 01600 891063
Boat excursions on the river Wye.

Amazing Hedge Puzzle & Butterfly Zoo

Jubilee Park, Whitchurch
☎ 01600 890360
A large hedge maze set on the
banks of the River Wye near
Symonds Yat.

Symonds Yat West Amusement Park

☎ 01600 890770
All weather facilities, inside
amusements.

The Wye Valley and Chepstow

Tourist Information

Castle car park
☎ 01291 623772

The Nurtons Gardens

Tintern
☎ 01291 689253
Open: Mar–Oct, Wed-Sun 11am-5pm

Tintern Abbey (English Heritage)

On A466, 7 miles north of Chepstow.
☎ 01291 689251
Evocative ruins of 13th-century Cistercian abbey.

Tintern station

Off A466, 7 miles north of Chepstow.
☎ 01291 689566
Restored station on former Wye Valley Railway line, with exhibits and refreshments.

Wynd Cliff

Off A466 2 miles north of Chepstow.
Fine viewpoint, picnic site, walks (including '365 steps').

Veddw House Garden

Devauden, nr Chepstow.
☎ 01291 650836
Open: Jun–Aug, Sun & BH Mon 2pm-5pm

Parva Farm Vineyard

Tintern NP16 6SQ
☎ 01291 689636

Chepstow Museum

Bridge Street, Chepstow
☎ 01291 625981
Past life and commercial activity of the town

Chepstow Castle (Cadw)

Bridge Street, Chepstow
☎ 01291 624065
Extensive ruins impressively sited overloking river Wye.

Caldicot Castle & Country Park

Church Road, Caldicot, 6 miles south-west of Chepstow.
☎ 01291 420421
Caldicot Castle is set in fifty five acres of beautiful Country Park.

Severnwye Llama & Camel Trekking

Sedbury, Chepstow
☎ 01291 621593
Llama and Camel trekking centre.

Caerwent

6 miles west of Chepstow on A48. Roman town, extensive walls and foundations of temple.

Dewstow Gardens & Grottoes

☎ 01291 430444
Open: Apr–Aug, Thu-Sun & BHs 10am-4.30pm
Monmouthshire's lost garden.

Places to Visit

Usk

Rural Life Museum

The Malt Barn, New Market Street, Usk.
☎ 01291 673777
Wide-ranging displays of local agricultural and social history.

Gwent Grass Ski Centre

Llanllywel, Usk
☎ 01291 672652

Raglan Castle (Cadw)

Off A40, 6 miles north of Usk.
☎ 01443 336000
Remains of impressive 15th-century castle, including Great Tower and suites of state apartments.

Llandegfedd Reservoir

4 miles west of Usk.
Sailing, boats for hire. Farm park adjacent.

Coleford

Tourist Information

High Street, Coleford
☎ 01594 812388
7 Church Street, Newent
☎ 01531 822468

Beechenhurst

Forestry Commission sculpture trail and other forest walks
Speech House Road, Broadwell, Coleford.
☎ 01594 827357

Cyril Hart Arboretum

Off B4226 east of Coleford, by Speech House.
☎ 01594 833057

Hopewell Colliery

Forest of Dean coal mining museum.
Off B4226 east of Coleford.
☎ 01594 810706

Clearwell Caves

Ancient iron mine and caves. Plus 'Iron Age Experience'.
The Rocks, Clearwell, Coleford
☎ 01594 832535

Perrygrove Railway

Narrow gauge steam railway, plus other attractions.
Perrygrove Road, Coleford.
☎ 01594 834991

Puzzle Wood

Pre-Roman open cast iron ore mine. Including unusual maze.
Coleford.
☎ 01594 833187

Cinderford & Lydney

Palace Theatre

Belle Vue Road, Cinderford.
☎ 01594 822555
Beautifully restored Edwardian theatre, mainly films.

Dean Heritage Centre

Mill, Soudley, Cinderford.
☎ 01594 822170

Museum portraying the life and culture of the Forest of Dean. Camp

Soudley Ponds

Soudley, Cinderford
☎ 01594 833057
Forestry Commission picnic site with pools and viewpoint.

Forest of Dean Mechanical Organs

Springfields, Drybrook, 3 miles north of Cinderford.
☎ 01594 542278
Mechanical organ museum.

Littledean Hall

On southern edge of Littledean, 1 mile east of Cinderford.
☎ 01594 824213
Reputedly England's oldest inhabited house. Exhibits include a packaging collection and Roman temple site.

Littledean Jail

At Littledean, 1 mile east of Cinderford.
☎ 01594 826659
18th-century pioneering prison, very little changed. Exhibitions, including 'Crime through Time' collection.

Dick Whittington Farm Park

Blakemore Farm, Little London, Longhope, 5 miles north-east of Cinderford.
☎ 01452 831000
Countryside centre with play barn and animals.

Elton Farm Mazes & Mountainboard Centre

Elton Farm, Elton, Newnham, 3 miles south-east of Cinderford. Mazes covering 8 acres, plus mountainboarding.

Forest Model Village

Lydney Park Estate, Old Park, Lydney.
☎ 01594 842244
Model village displaying forest scenes and people.

Nagshead Nature Reserve

Fancy Road, Parkend, Lydney.
☎ 01594 833057
RSPB Nature Reserve with trails and visitor centre.

Lydney Park Spring Gardens

Lydney Park Estate, Lydney. Gloucestershire,
☎ 01594 842844
Spring Gardens with rhododendrons and azaleas. Roman temple site and museum.

Dean Forest Railway

Forest Road, Lydney.
☎ 01594 843423
Preserved steam railway running between Lydney Junction and Parkend. Displays and other attractions.

This final chapter covers an area spanning the border and centred on the Black Mountains and their associated valleys.

Abergavenny, Hay and the Black Mountains

Rhydspence

Whitney tollbridge

A438

B4352

Arthur's Stone

Moccas Park

Clyro

B4348

A438

Hay-on-Wye

Dorestone

R. Wye

Hereford

Glasbury

B4348

Peterchurch

B4349

Vowchurch

GOLDEN VALLEY

R. Dore

B4347

THE BLACK MOUNTAINS

A4078

Talgarth

Trefecca

Capel-y-ffin

Abbey Dore Court Gardens

Llanthony Priory

Abbey Dore

A465

Kilpeck

VALE OF EWYAS

Longtown

Pontrilas

A479

Llangorse

Waun Fach 811m

Llanthony

Grosmont Castle

Cwmyoy

Grosmont

Skenfrith Castle

Pandy

Penallt-mawr 720m

A40

Tretower Castle and Court

Pen Cerrig Calch

Llanfihangel Crucorney

Skenfrith

Crickhowell

A40

Sugar Loaf 596m

Ysgyryd Fawr 485m

White Castle

B4347

B4521

0   5 miles

0   7Km

Abergavenny

B4233

Llanvapley

Rockfield

This is a romantic countryside of isolated small towns and remote villages, and in the past it has nurtured some equally romantic personalities. The great central mass of hills dictates the boundaries of the area and gives it unity. The Welsh border divides it on the map, but it has never had much practical significance.

This point is illustrated very soon after you leave Hereford on the A465, because almost at once you enter a part of Herefordshire full of Welsh place names. This is the territory known in post-Norman times as Archenfield. For 200 years after the Conquest, it remained a pocket of Welshness in an otherwise English environment. The inhabitants had a reputation for extreme loyalty to the English crown – in fact they had the 'privilege' of forming the vanguard of the English armies in their campaigns against the Welsh. In return the people were allowed to observe Welsh law and customs. Needless to say, they were regarded as traitors by other Welshmen, who extracted revenge whenever possible. Even today, the area has a distinctive atmosphere of 'no-man's-land', consisting of scattered farms and tiny hamlets, with churches often isolated from any settlement.

The first feature of interest is off the A465 about ten miles out of Hereford. Take the road to the left about a mile after the village of Didley (signposted 'Kilpeck') and pass the solitary church of St Devereux to reach **Kilpeck,** which is an attractive mixture of stone and timber-frame houses. What attracts thousands of visitors (and many scholars) each year is the small sandstone church, which many believe to be the most remarkable in Britain. Norman in origin, it has a profusion of carving, the work of the anonymous men who formed what has come to be known as the Herefordshire School of Carving. Their work is widespread throughout the county, but at Kilpeck they excelled themselves, producing a riot of decoration in many moods – moral, religious, historical and frivolous. Every aspect of medieval life is depicted here, both inside and outside the church. Other features to note are the enormous font and the tub-like stoup with carved hands clasped round it.

The Golden Valley

From Kilpeck return to the main road and move on to Pontrilas. The right turn here on to the B4347 is the way into the **Golden Valley,** a name which has a disappointingly prosaic origin - at some point the Welsh 'dwr' (water) became confused with 'd'or' (golden). The valley is over twelve miles long and forms the course of the river Dore, which rises above Hay-on-Wye.

The first village encountered, **Ewyas Harold**, is not exactly beautiful or impressive, although at the time of the Doomsday Book it was one of only five boroughs in the county, and there are records of merchants from France visiting its fairs in the fourteenth century. Nowadays it has a modern, functional appearance, and the only reminder of its former importance is the castle mound. The recently-built Roman Catholic church is in some ways more interesting than the parish church, although the latter has a memorial that has puzzled people for a long time. It is of fourteenth century origin and shows a woman holding a heart in her hands.

The famous **Abbey Dore** is a few minutes' drive further up the valley road. The big church is all that remains of the Cistercian Abbey, but it is impressive nevertheless, mainly because you do not expect to see such a large building standing in very ordinary fields. When Henry VIII dissolved the great monastic houses, Abbey Dore came into the hands of the Scudamore family, and the first Viscount commissioned the famous carpenter John Abel to restore it from its ruinous condition. In the process over 200 tons of oak were used in the roof, and the twelfth-century altar was retrieved from a farmyard. It was re-consecrated in 1634. One of its outstanding features is the substantial and elaborate chancel screen carved by Abel himself. Nearby is **Abbey Dore Court** where the gardens are open to the public.

It is worth turning left after Abbey Dore to visit the churches at **Bacton** and **St Margaret's**. There is nothing very remarkable about Bacton church itself, but it is noted for an effigy of Blanche Parry, lady-in-waiting to Elizabeth I. She took on her duties when the future Queen was only three years old and remained in royal service for the rest of her life. It condemned her, of course, to spinsterhood, a fact which is much praised in the accompanying inscription. It is said that one of the church's treasures, an elaborately-embroidered altar frontal, is Blanche Parry's work.

You reach **St Margaret's** by climbing steeply out of Bacton. John Betjeman recalled a visit here: '*My own memory of the perfect Herefordshire is a spring day in the foothills of the Black Mountains and finding among the winding hilltop lanes the remote little church of St. Margaret's where there was no sound but a farm dog's distant barking. Opening the church door I saw across the whole width of the little chancel a screen and loft all delicately carved and textured pale grey with time*'. Nothing much has changed. From the outside the church looks unpromisingly plain, standing in a roughly-mown field. It is an exposed spot, commanding wide views, but it was precisely this remoteness that saved the magnificent rood screen from destruction after the Reformation. The wall texts are another notable feature, and they are now bright and clean after restoration. The one over the door as you leave says dauntingly 'Go and sin no more'. The intricate screen conceals the Norman chancel arch, to one side of which is a stone staircase leading to the rood loft. The church richly repays the tortuous drive.

Soon after returning to the main road you cross the river and also the track of the old railway that once linked Hay with the Hereford-Abergavenny line. At **Vowchurch** you have the odd prospect of two churches facing each other across the river and separated by a few hundred yards. The one on the opposite bank belongs to the tiny hamlet of Turnastone. Vowchurch's own parish church is unusual for having its roof supported on wooden posts set in the walls. Poston camp, to the north-west, is one of the few hill forts in the border country to have been systematically investigated, and the finds have included some rare first-century native pottery. To the east is Monnington Court (not open), built near the site of a house once occupied by the Scudamore family in which Owain Glyndwr took refuge with his daughter-in-law just before his death.

Peterchurch is the unofficial 'capital' of the valley in that it has a secondary school and also the finest parish church. The spire is plastic (the original fourteenth-century one was taken down some years ago) but the rest of the church is genuine and rather unusual inside, where three arches of decreasing height divide the church down its length. Another interesting feature is the memorial on the wall showing a carp with a chain round its neck, alleged to commemorate the catching of a fish in St Peter's Well nearby. Wellbrook Manor

Above: Abbey Dore

(not open), a short distance east of the church, is a famous example of a hall-house of the fourteenth century, being partly of cruck construction and with its timber-framing cased in stone.

Dorstone lies at the head of the valley, one of the many border settlements which failed to develop into boroughs. It has the characteristic sequence of castle, market-place and church, although only the motte and bailey remain of the castle, and the church was largely rebuilt in 1889. Richard de Brito, one of the knights who murdered Thomas a Becket, came here after completing a period of penance in Palestine. He founded a chapel in the church in 1256, as recorded on a stone found during the rebuilding. Another building of interest in Dorstone is the school on the south side of the market place, founded in 1643 to provide a free education for the village children.

The site of the original terminus of the Golden Valley railway can still be traced on the edge of the village by the river bridge. It was opened in 1881, but was wildly unprofitable, even after it had been extended to Hay in 1889. The passenger service ceased in 1941 and the line was closed altogether in 1957.

Dorstone is best known for the burial chamber known as **Arthur's Stone**, which can be reached by a track leading off the main road a little way north-east of the village. The connection with Arthur is dubious, but the tomb, with its huge capstone, is a remarkable structure, estimated as being of Neolithic origin. Until the mid-nineteenth century, it was the gathering-place for village celebrations.

The return to Pontrilas can be made either on the same road or by a series of rather more interesting minor roads over the hills to the west. If you decide on the latter you should leave Dorstone on the Snodhill road. **Snodhill,** about a mile to the south, is famous because of an entertaining description in the diary of the Reverend Francis Kilvert of a typically elaborate Victorian picnic on its castle site. This extends to about ten acres with some substantial remains, and is still a good place for a picnic. One of the features of the village is the number of farmsteads with the local sandstone roof cladding.

You go south from Snodhill on a narrow road that rises and falls steeply in places. Standing isolated at the side of the road after about three miles is the **Urishay chapel,** probably Norman in origin, with the site of the castle which it served next to it. The remains of a large seventeenth-century house now stand on the motte. There are fine views from here, but it remains a rather desolate spot. After another three miles turn right at the crossroads to reach the hamlet of **Michaelchurch Escley,** where it is worth visiting the church to see the large wall painting, a traditional representation of Christ of the Trades showing Christ surrounded by an assortment of tools.

You now follow the lonely road that runs by the Escley Brook down to **Longtown.** The main village is on another road over to the right, and the fact that there is a mountain rescue post is a reminder that just to the west are some of the most formidable areas of the Black Mountains. There are two castles at Longtown. One, simply a motte and bailey, is situated out of the village to the south, where the Olchon Brook joins the river Monnow. The other is at the northern end and has some interesting ruins. Moving south again, you very quickly reach **Clodock.** The church here was founded, according to

Above left: The three Tri-lateral Castles, Skenfrith Castle; middle: White Castle. right: Grosmont Castle.

The Tri-lateral Castles

legend, when Clydawg, King of Ewyas, was murdered on a hunting expedition in 540. The oxen drawing the cart with his body on it refused to cross the ford here, so the King was buried nearby. The church was built on the spot and dedicated to him. It is a fascinating building with some seventeenth-century box pews, a three-decker pulpit, a musicians' gallery and a rare example of a three-sided communion rail.

Make sure you take the road on the west of the river when you leave Clodock, since the route on the other side is complicated, to say the least. You emerge on to the A465 at **Pandy** after a tour that has taken in some of the remotest Herefordshire countryside. The river Monnow, which now takes in the river Honddu, curves away east and goes on to achieve a respectable size as it flows through Monmouth and Chepstow to the Severn estuary.

It is worth pointing out here that one of the highest and loneliest stretches of the Offa's Dyke path starts at Pandy and continues along the ridges of the Black Mountains to Hay. It is a potentially dangerous walk, definitely for the experienced only, and the usual precautions should be taken before starting on it. You reach it by a turning opposite the Lancaster Arms in Pandy.

The Tri-lateral Castles

The countryside to the south of the Golden Valley is not so exciting scenically, but it is rich in interest. Pontrilas is again the starting point. Take the B4347 down the Monnow valley for

Grosmont, which has one of the 'Trilateral' castles, a group of three situated around Graig Syfyrddu, the others being Skenfrith and White Castle. Grosmont village is a comfortable, lived-in place, with the church and castle standing on opposite sides of the main street. It is surprising, on entering the church, to step into what appears at first to be a dim lumber-room with a rough floor and two rows of arches. This is, in fact, the nave of the church. The building was originally of a size designed to indicate the importance of Grosmont. Unfortunately it was always too big for the congregation, and as the numbers of worshippers declined further, only the chancel was used for services. When the church was restored in 1870, a glazed screen was put up to shut off the nave entirely, and now the contrast between the rough austerity of the nave and the richness of the chancel is startling. The castle, impressively situated on a rounded hill above a deep moat, has a keep, a gatehouse and high curtain walls, but the most unusual feature is the delicate fourteenth-century chimney, a relic of the banqueting hall.

Continuing down the road with Garway Hill on the left, you arrive at Skenfrith Castle after about three miles. **Skenfrith**, now an attractive village, was one of many places in the border which started promisingly as settlements but failed to survive, in this case owing to the increasing prominence of its neighbour Grosmont, which acquired the vital market. The castle is the least impressive of the three and was never of major military importance, although John of Gaunt was once Governor. It has an extensive round keep within a bailey with towers at each corner. The sandstone church has a heavily-buttressed tower and a fine 'double-decker' belfry, and the interior is of interest, with memorials to the Morgan family. Their seventeenth-century pew can still be seen. The church's main treasure, however, is an embroidered fifteenth-century cope.

A further three miles to the south, **Rockfield** is the estate village of Rockfield House, the home of the Rolls family, whose best-known member was the Hon. Charles, co-founder of Rolls-Royce. You turn right here on to the Abergavenny road and follow it to Llantilio Crossenny, where a right turn leads up to **White Castle**. The name is a reminder that these castles looked a little different in the middle ages when they were coated with primitive paint or plaster and must have gleamed in the sun. It is the best-preserved of the Trilateral castles, though unlike the other two it has no accompanying settlement. The remains include inner and outer wards, a towered gatehouse and moats.

The hill to the west of White Castle, dominating the whole landscape is **Ysgyryd Fawr (or Skirrid)**. It is National Trust property, and the best way to reach the top is to continue north from White Castle, turn left on to the B4521 and follow it to a point about two miles from Abergavenny when you are right under the hill. There is a lay-by on the right, and a little further on a National Park boundary sign by a stile. The walk is waymarked from here and proceeds through a plantation to the southern end of the hill, where a path continues to the summit at 1596ft. Skirrid is a hill of great religious significance. To the west of the summit is a huge cleft, caused, according to legend, by the hill splitting when the veil of the temple was rent at the Crucifixion. The trigonometrical point at the top stands in the still-traceable ruins of a chapel dedicated to St Michael, which received papal approval as an object of pilgrimage.

The Vale of Ewyas

It is time now to explore the second and most dramatic of the Black Mountain valleys - the Honddu valley, or **Vale of Ewyas**. Access is via Llanfihangel Crucorny on the A465, where the B4423 turns into the Vale. A word of warning: this road starts as a broad highway but very soon narrows, and in the peak holiday season it can be notoriously congested. One reason for the traffic is that the road becomes a scenic drive to Hay at the northern end of the Vale, and it is a good idea to come here early in the morning or in the evening.

Llanfihangel Crucorny is worth stopping to see. The Skirrid Inn is supposedly Norman in origin, but its present structure is medieval. Its most interesting feature is its oak staircase (you will have to ask permission to see it), where sheep-stealers were apparently lynched when the building was a courthouse. This is an area of curious and highly individual churches, and one of the remotest and most rewarding is **Partrishow**. About a mile and a half up the Ewyas Valley road from Llanfihangel Crucorny there is a left turn which takes you through near-deserted countryside to the little church, most famous for its superb rood loft and screen, but containing several other

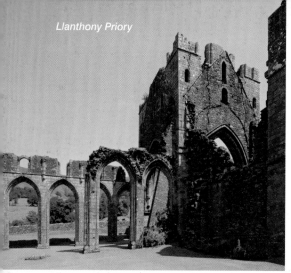

along the outside of the church facing the churchyard cross are a reminder that local affairs were once formally discussed at the cross. Close by is a stone hut with a fireplace where the priest could thaw out before taking the service.

Also highly individual is the church at **Cwmyoy**, about two miles further up the valley road. It stands in an isolated position on the east side of the river, and there are two approach roads; you are strongly advised to take the second turning through Neuadd farm, then leave the car at the first opportunity and walk. There is hardly any parking space at the church itself. It has been in the past the victim of landslip, with the result that its tower and walls lean in all directions, supported by heavy buttresses. The effect is even more

features of interest, including a 'memento mori' (a representation of Death as a skeleton) and three altar tables dating from before the Reformation. One of them is in a small cell at the west end. The inscription on the large font refers to Cynhillin, Prince of Powys just before the Norman Conquest, and seems to date it as eleventh century. Stone benches

Tretower Castle & Manor House

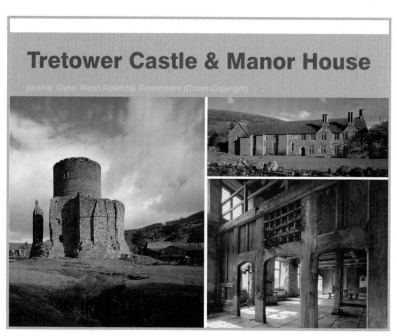

Above: The River Wye, Glasbury

Above: Castle Bookshop, Hay-on-Wye

alarming inside, where there is hardly a perpendicular wall. If one disregards all this, the interior is superb. The tiny chancel and sanctuary are at a much higher level than the nave; combined with the effect of the low roof, this gives the east end a peculiarly intimate atmosphere. Look at the churchyard, too. The gravestones are fine examples of the local stonemason's art, and there is a moving memorial to Jane Thomas and her baby at the southeast corner of the church, close to the old churchyard cross. The hummocks of the landslip are still very much in evidence above the church.

As you return to the valley road and drive towards **Llanthony Priory**, the rocky outcrops above Cwmyoy and the bleak summits on both sides of the road leave no doubt as to why a religious order seeking total seclusion should have selected this valley as the site for a priory. Until fairly recently, access to the further reaches of this valley were difficult and often impossible in winter, and not very easy in a wet summer. A group of Augustinian monks formed a community at Llanthony at the beginning of the twelfth century, but it was not long before local warfare between the Welsh and the Normans drove them away in search of security. They established a new home, called Llanthony Secunda, near Gloucester, and although a fresh start was made in the Vale of Ewyas in about 1175 there was continual rivalry between the old and new establishments. The two became independent in 1205, but it was the Gloucester community which flourished, with the result that it received royal authority in 1481 to take over the older priory, which was by now almost deserted. When both communities were dissolved in 1538, Llanthony fell into private hands and little was done to maintain it. A shooting lodge was built into the ruins at the beginning of the nineteenth century, and in 1807 the whole place was bought by the poet Walter Savage Landor, who had ambitious plans to develop the estate. Living temporarily in the shooting lodge, he started to build a house above the ruins, but intense local hostility and a stream of litigation forced him to leave, virtually bankrupt, in 1815. A special fund was set up to pay for the restoration of the ruins, but it was not until the 1930s that systematic work began.

In recent years the shooting lodge has become a small hotel, but the remaining ruins can be visited, preferably out of season or late in the evening, when something of the atmosphere that attracted the original settlers can still be sensed. The ruins mainly comprise the two magnificent towers of the west end, a centre tower and the north nave arcade. The gatehouse stands apart from the main site close to the road. The long, low building that was probably once the infirmary is now the parish church of St David, the plain interior of which is relieved by a remarkable group of slate memorial tablets on each side of the chancel, and it is pleasant to see the old oil lamps still in position. A short walk above the priory is waymarked. It passes some of the woodland planted by Landor and also the remains of his ill-fated house. The start of the walk is the field at the back of the ruins.

Four miles further on is **Capel-y-Ffin**, 'The Chapel on the Boundary', which has a romantic history involving The Revd Joseph Leycester Lyne, who was ordained as a deacon in the Anglican Church in 1860 and began a self-imposed task of re-establishing English monasticism. Calling himself Father Ignatius, he attempted to acquire Llanthony Priory for this purpose, but having failed he decided to build a monastery from scratch at Capel-y-Ffin. By means of a series of preaching tours he raised enough money to start building in 1870. His charismatic personality was sufficient to attract recruits, and the establishment survived rather precariously until 1908, when he died. His successors failed to achieve the drive and fund-raising successes of the founder, and the community eventually linked itself with a monastery on the island of Caldy, whose members entered the Roman Catholic Church in 1913.

Opinions differed sharply on the subject of Father Ignatius, but there is little doubt that he was a sincere and idealistic man who failed to see that his unorthodox methods could be misunderstood, both locally and further afield. All that now remains of the monastery church is the roofless nave and chancel containing the grave slab of Father Ignatius, maintained by a Memorial Trust set up in 1968. The residential quarters, privately owned, are nearby. They were bought in 1924 by the sculptor and designer Eric Gill with the aim of setting up another community, this time of artists. This venture also failed, mainly because of the poor communications in the valley.

To visit the remains of the monastery church, take the minor road to the left in Capel-y-Ffin for a few hundred yards and cross the stile set into a stone archway on the left. The path up to the buildings is short but very steep. Before you go do not miss the little eighteenth-century church in Capel-y-Ffin with its odd leaning belfry. It may well be the smallest you will ever see, but even so it has a miniature west gallery and shows every sign of being well cared for. The Baptist chapel, very similar in style, is beyond it on the other side of the stream.

The road north of Capel-y-Ffin winds its way to a cattle grid and then suddenly emerges on to magnificent open mountainside, providing at long last a chance to park and look at the view back down the valley. You then drive through the Gospel Pass and emerge on to **Hay Bluff**, where there is one of the most magnificent panoramas to be found in these parts. The descent to Hay-on-Wye begins here. Hay is described later in the chapter, and for the moment we return to the the A465 at the bottom of the valley to visit **Abergavenny**.

On to Abergavenny

As you approach the town you are struck at once by the hills that surround it. Immediately ahead is the looming Blorenge, and it is hard to believe that on the other side of it are the industrial valleys of South Wales. Equally prominent on the right is the Sugar Loaf, and between them lies the Usk Valley. A glance at the map shows that the valley is a strategic route into central Wales, so Abergavenny, at its head, has always been of historical importance. The Romans had a fortress here called Gobanium, a motte and bailey was built around 1100, and a more substantial castle was erected in the twelfth century.

In summer, Abergavenny has the bustling air of a tourist centre, but out of season it becomes the sort of border town with which we are now familiar - grey, rather drab, not caring too much about appearances and generally carrying out the unromantic but necessary functions of a rural centre. Even so, it has an honourable place in Welsh cultural history because it was here that the Welsh Literary Society was founded in 1833, meeting at the Sun Inn. The annual Eisteddfod which resulted was held for 21 years, and was a vital factor in encouraging the revival of the Welsh language.

The main street is dominated at its top end by the huge **Town Hall and Market**, complete with clock tower, a grandiose Victorian complex that includes a theatre.. The gem of the street is undoubtedly the Angel Hotel, early nineteenth-century, but looking older. The **castle** is at the bottom end, and what remains of it has a very placid air, since the grounds have been tidied up to the point where neatness has taken away any impressiveness the site may once have had. What appears to be a keep in a remarkable state of preservation, is in fact, an early-Victorian shooting lodge, now in service as the **town museum,** featuring local memorabilia and offering free admission. Nearby are the tranquil **Linda Vista Gardens and Castle Meadows.**

The **Church of St Mary** is all that survives of the great Benedictine Priory established by Hamelin de Ballon soon after the Conquest. It is a cathedral-like building, remarkable for the large number of memorials, mainly commemorating the families of Marcher lords, but its outstanding feature is an immense effigy of Jesse, father of David, carved from a single piece of oak and possibly of fourteenth-century origin. The medieval choir stalls are also worthy of note. Unfortunately, the church is normally kept locked on most weekdays, and if you wish to see the interior you will need to contact the local information centre in advance to discover the current arrangements. At the side of the church a cavernous tithe barn still stands, used now as commercial premises. The town has other buildings of interest tucked away, and a 'town trail' is available either at the Museum or at the excellent **Information Centre** by the bus station in Monmouth Road. This is also the Brecon Beacons National Park Centre and well worth a visit, particularly to find some useful walking guides.

The walk to the summit of the **Sugar Loaf** has long been a favourite excursion, and the easiest way is to leave the town on the A40 and after about a mile turn right into a road signposted 'Sugar Loaf'. You eventually reach a car park from which the final ascent of nearly two miles can be made.

On to Hay-on-Wye

The route out of Abergavenny is the A40 along the Usk valley, passing after four miles the former depot of the South Wales Borderers and the Prince of Wales' Division. **Crickhowell**, two miles further on, lies under the distinctive flat-topped hill known as 'Table Mountain'. The slight remains of its castle are incorporated into a park on the left as you enter from this direction. The tiny square has the decorative Bear Hotel on one side; on the other, the High Street leads away towards the river and continues as Bridge Street, a most attractive hill with some well-maintained small houses. The 13-arch stone bridge with pedestrian alcoves is the pride of Crickhowell, and the river can be an exciting sight here when it is in full spate. You get a good view of the town from the bridge, and the church is particularly prominent. If you walk back up by the main road instead of Bridge Street, you can see at the top an impressive old wall with a gatehouse. This is Forth Mawr, and used to be the entrance to an important Tudor house belonging to the Herbert family. Unfortunately the house has been long since demolished. If you want to climb Table Mountain the best way is probably via the lane at Glannant, half a mile out of Crickhowell on the A40. The large white house visible to the north-west here is Gwernvale, the birthplace of Sir George Everest, who was the first to map accurately the position of the mountain to which he gave his name.

Two miles beyond Crickhowell the road forks and you take the A479, which quickly brings you to **Tretower**. From the main road you can see at once the castle and manor house down on the left. The castle was once of great importance, lying as it did at the junction of routes west to Brecon and north to Hay. Originally made of wood, it was surrounded by a stone curtain wall in the twelfth century, and, not long after, the old buildings were replaced by the present circular tower. A little later still, the adjoining Tretower Court was built, presumably to provide more comfortable accommodation. The buildings are open to the public. Before going in, notice the fine restored stone barn opposite the gateway; inside, the castle has become inextricably mixed up with a farm, which somehow seems preferable to the neat municipalisation at Abergavenny.

Soon after Tretower the hills begin to close in on each side of the road. Pen Tir and the Mynydd Troed range on the left are very prominent, while high up on the right is the craggy escarpment of Mynydd Llysiau at over two thousand feet. Then the countryside suddenly opens up at Pengenffordd and there is a gentle descent into **Talgarth,** where the once-congested streets have been relieved by a by-pass.

The car park here is in what was once the station yard, and traces of the old Brecon, Hay and Hereford railway, mentioned often in the Kilvert Diaries, can still be seen. Three miles north, near Three Cocks, was a junction with a line that ran up the Wye valley and on past Rhayader. Talgarth is rather austere, although picturesque enough with its steep and narrow streets. One interesting feature in the square is a medieval tower and guardhouse by the bridge, with a shop and bank neatly fitted into it. The church, dedicated, unusually, to St Gwendoline, is at the north-east edge of the town and here there is a very significant memorial to **Howell Harris,** born nearby at Trefecca in 1713.

The story of Howell Harris and the

'Family' is a fascinating one, too long to be told in full here. He was the founder of the Calvinistic Methodist Church of Wales and led a tough life of preaching, often at odds with the Church of England and rival Nonconformist sects. Later in life he decided to establish a community, or Family, for his followers, who would give up their possessions and become self-supporting. He set it up at Trefecca, and, surprisingly, it was a success, spreading to nearly eight hundred acres and proving to be well in the forefront of agricultural development at that time. Among other things Harris introduced into Wales the use of root crops as fodder and helped to found the Brecknockshire Agricultural Society, the first of its kind in Britain. Shortly before his death in 1773, a training college for ministers was added to the community. The buildings are still there, just over a mile to the south along the B4560, and the chapel block now houses an interesting Harris museum.

On the eastern side of the bridge at Talgarth a lane leads to **Llanelieu**, the site of another isolated and fascinating church. It is a simple building in a fine setting. Its most interesting feature is the roughly-carved rood screen, rather less sophisticated than others in this area but adding much to the austere and remote atmosphere of the church. If it is locked, the key can normally be obtained from the farm close by.

If you visit Trefecca it is worth continuing south to **Llangorse lake**. Not so long ago, it was a lonely, romantic stretch of water supposedly concealing a submerged town, but in recent years it has attracted camping and caravan sites, a holiday adventure centre and various water sports facilities. Visited out of season it provides much of interest in the way of wildlife. A waymarked path round the western side links Llangorse in the north with Llangasty in the south.

Across the river from Talgarth is **Bronllys,** noted for a church with a very odd detached tower and also for its big hospital, built with funds raised as a memorial to Edward VII. The castle here consists of little more than a high circular tower dating from the mid-thirteenth century. Access to the main chamber is possible by way of a wooden staircase, and the basement and dungeon can be inspected from above, but there is no way to the top.

The A4078 out of Talgarth leads on to Three Cocks and **Glasbury,** where you begin to enter the Kilvert country. **Francis Kilvert**, born in Wiltshire, became the curate of Clyro, near Hay-on-Wye, in 1865. He was a conscientious young man, spending many hours walking the area on his visits to parishioners, while recording his experiences in a diary. When the diaries were published just before the Second World War, they were recognised at once not only as a literary classic but as a valuable source of social history. The young, susceptible clergyman brought a fresh and observant eye to the comings and goings in his part of the countryside, and the Diaries give a unique insight into the life and work of people in the neighbourhood, from the wealthiest to the poorest. In 1877 he became Vicar of Bredwardine and Rector of Brobury, Herefordshire (about eight miles east of Hay-on-Wye), and two years later married Elizabeth Rowland. Soon after their return from honeymoon, however, he fell ill with peritonitis and died. He is buried in St Andrew's churchyard, Bredwardine. Unfortunately, after his death his widow destroyed much of his work, but the Diaries have remained popular, and each year people come to Clyro to retrace Kilvert's walks and visits, and a Society exists to encourage this interest.

The bridge at Glasbury marks the reunion with the river Wye, and this village has suffered more than most during its history from severe flooding. This explains the fact that the church is a long way from the village, the first building having been washed away. Its replacement was built out of harm's way in 1664, but the present church is a new version, built on the same site in 1836.

After crossing the river at Glasbury and continuing on the A438 you see after a mile a left turn signposted 'Mae-syronnen Chapel'. This is one of the very earliest places of Nonconformist worship in Wales – a low, single-storey building with a tiny cottage at one end. It may be locked, but by peering through the windows you can see that much of the original furnishing remains, including the extremely un-comfortable wooden benches. Nearby **Llowes** has a church notable for its Celtic Cross and a common that was one of Kilvert's favourite walks.

From here it is three miles to **Clyro**, which seems to have changed remark-ably little since Kilvert's time, apart from the by-pass, which has taken the traffic out of the village but is a visual intru-sion. As you turn off into the village, you see on the other side of the by-pass

the old school where Kilvert taught. To find his lodgings you turn right at the church gate. The house, once known as Ty Dulas and now called Ashbrook, currently houses an art gallery, but also has Kilvert memorabilia. The Basker-ville Arms, frequently mentioned by Kilvert who used its old name, the Swan, still stands opposite, and the noise is no doubt just as irritating to the present occupiers of Ashbrook as it was to him.

In Kilvert's day a trip to **Hay-on-Wye** was a major expedition for the inhabitants of Clyro, but now it is a few minutes' drive across the bridge. Opinions differ on the subject of Hay. For some people it is an undistinguished jumble of nondescript architecture and claustrophobic streets; for others it is the perfect small town with an intimate and convivial atmosphere. It does give the impression of being built on a mini-ature scale, and there is a strong sense of a medieval town huddling at the foot of its castle.

Not so long ago Hay was like most other small border towns – a rural shopping centre and market. Now it has achieved wider fame as the world capital of the second-hand book trade. Richard Booth first set up a bookshop in the Castle in the early 1960s and gradually extended his empire to the former cinema and fire station. Other dealers caught on, with the result that the book trade now dominates the town. This led naturally to the emergence of the prestigious annual Literary Festival, when the great and good of the book world come to meet their admirers.

The Castle' – the residence of

Richard Booth, the unofficial King of Hay – is something of a misnomer. Very few traces remain of the Norman structure, and the building that occupies the site is a seventeenth-century mansion, occupied in Kilvert's time by the Bevan family with whom he spent a good deal of time. The motte of a smaller and earlier castle can be seen between the town centre and the rather distant church of St Mary, which was almost entirely rebuilt in 1834. The modern bridge is the latest of a series since 1763 which have been destroyed by flooding, ice or other disasters. The Wye has proved a mixed blessing, although it was once a source of commercial prosperity for the town. There is now an attractive walk along its bank, reached by a path near the church.

Hay is undoubtedly one of the best touring centres in the border region, lying as it does at the meeting-place of three characteristic border landscapes – the mountains to the south, the Radnor moorlands to the north, and the rich Herefordshire countryside to the west.

Places to Visit

The Black Mountains Valleys

Kilpeck Church

Off A465, 8 miles southwest of Hereford.
Profuse Norman carving, inside and out, and other features of interest.

Grosmont church

On B4347 (off A465), 3 miles south of Pontrilas.
Unusual church with elegant chancel and impressive 'abandoned' nave.

Grosmont Castle

On B4347 (off A465), 3 miles south of Pontrilas.
Moated castle with keep and other remains. Open access.

Skenfrith Castle

Off B4347, 7 miles south-east of Pontrilas.
Substantial remains, including keep and defensive walls. Open access. Neighbouring church of interest.

White Castle (Cadw)

Off B452, 4 miles west of
Abergavenny.
☎ 01600 780380
Open: Apr–Sep, Wed-Sun & BH
Mon. 10am-5pm. Other times free.
Extensive ruins, including moat,
drawbridge, keep. Open access.
Interesting church at Llanvetherine.

In the Golden Valley:

Dore Abbey

In Golden Valley. On B4347, 11
miles south-west of Hereford.
Surviving church of Cistercian
abbey. Fine roof work and carved
screen.

St Margaret's Church

On minor roads 4 miles north-west
of Dore Abbey
Remote church, impressively sited,
with superb oak rood screen and
wall texts.

Arthur's Stone

At head of Golden Valley on B4347.
Neolithic burial chamber above
Dorstone.

In the Vale of Ewyas:

Partrishow Church

Turn off the valley road about 1 mile
north-west of Llanfihangel Crucorny
– OS map advisable.
Probably the best of the remote
and 'untouched' churches in the
area. Rood screen and loft and
much else of interest.

Cwmyoy church

On valley road off A465, 3
miles north west of Llanfihangel
Crucorny.
Famous 'leaning' church, victim of
landslip, but still in use.

Llanthony Priory (Cadw)

Infirmary. Free access.
On valley road off A465, 6 miles
north west of Llanfihangel Crucorny.
Substantial remains of isolated
Augustinian Priory of 11th and 12th
centuries. Also parish church in
former abbey building

Capel-y-Ffin

Remains of Llanthony 'Abbey',
founded by 'Father Ignatius', who
is buried there. Also picturesque
Anglican and Baptist chapels.
On valley road off A465, 12
miles north west of Llanfihangel
Crucorny.

Abergavenny

Tourist Information

Swan Meadow
☎ 01873 857588

Town Hall, Abergavenny

Interesting building housing big
indoor market and theatre.

Abergavenny Museum

In keep of Abergavenny Castle
Pictures, artefacts and memorabilia
relating to local history and life.
Children's activities. Art and craft
exhibitions. Free admission.

Places to Visit

Linda Vista Gardens, Abergavenny

Adjacent to castle.
Public gardens established in 1843. Floral displays, including orchids and shrubs.

Castle Meadows

Adjacent to castle.
Meadows offering pleasant riverside strolls.

Penpergwm Lodge Garden

Nr Abergavenny NP7 9AS
☎ 01873 840208
Open: Apr-Sep Thu-Sun 2pm-6pm

Priory church, Abergavenny

Church noted for its size and the number of its memorials.

Tretower Court (Cadw)

9 miles northwest of Abergavenny on A479.
www.cadw.wales.gov.uk
Restored 15th-century courtyard house with fine timberwork. Recreated fifteenth-century garden. (Admission charge includes Tretower Castle.) **Closed for conservation work during 2009, see website for details.**

Trefecca College

2 miles south of Talgarth on B4560. Religious study centre, formerly home of community set up by Howell Harris, nonconformist preacher and agricultural pioneer. Museum relating to Harris's life and work.

Hay-on-Wye

Bookshops

Hay is full of them, with Richard Booth's book 'empire' at their heart.

Clyro

Situated across the bridge from Hay.
The village where the famous diarist Francis Kilvert was curate from 1865 to 1872. His lodgings are still there (now an art gallery) as are many other buildings familiar to readers of the Diary.

Rhydspence Inn

3 miles north-east of Clyro on A438.
Famous old drover's inn situated on the border.

Maesyronnen Chapel

2 miles north of Glasbury.
One of the oldest places of Nonconformist worship in Wales, and still in use. Some original furniture.

Whitney-on-Wye Toll Bridge

On B4350 adjacent A438 near Rhydspence.
Distinctive bridge to Hay-on-Wye.

Accommodation

Tourist Information Centres have a booking bureau with the exception of Powys, where it is all handled by Brecon Tourist Information Centre (except for Presteigne, where they will handle bookings made in person at the centre).

Getting there

Airports

The main airports are Birmingham, Bristol and Cardiff

Bus/Coach

Regular coach services from around the country to the larger towns of the area. Enquires: National Express ☎ 08717 818181 or www.eurolines.co.uk" www.eurolines.co.uk

Car

M6 & M54 to Shrewsbury and then pick your route from the A5 Shrewsbury bypass; A-roads west from the M5 or M50 to Ross-on-Wye; M4 west bound and take M48 (the northern Severn Bridge for Chepstow); M4 east bound and the M48 to Chepstow.

Rail

There are regular services to Shrewsbury, Hereford, Gloucester and Chepstow. There are services between Gloucester and Chepstow; Hereford and Abergavenny; Hereford and Shrewsbury via Leominster; Shrewsbury and Builth Wells via Ludlow; Craven Arms to Church Stretton; Craven Arms to Knighton and Llandrindod Wells (including several small stations en-route); Craven Arms to Llandovery and Builth Wells; Shrewsbury to Aberystwyth, via Welshpool and Newtown.

Activities

Herefordshire

Golden Valley Llamas
Old King Street Farm, Ewyas Harold, Hereford HR2 0HB
☎ 01981 240208
www.goldenvalleyllamas.co.uk
Day and half-day llama treks

Paddles & Pedals Canoe Hire
15 Castle St, Hay-on-Wye HR3 5DF
☎ 01497 820604
www.paddlesandpedals.co.uk

Wheely Wonderful Cycling
☎ 01568 770755
www.wheelywonderfulcycling.co.uk
4 miles (6km) south-west of Ludlow

Wye Valley Canoes
The Boat House, Glasbury-on-Wye, Hereford HR3 5NP
☎ 847213
www.wyevalleycanoes.co.uk

Monmouthshire

Beacon Park Boats
The Boat House, Llanfoist Wharf,
Abergavenny NP7 9NG
☎ 01873 858277
www.beaconparkboats.com

Goytre Wharf Tourist Information Outlet
Llanover
☎ 01873 881069
Heritage, activity and study centre

Powys

Llangorse Multi-Activity Centre
Gilfach Farm, Llangorse, Brecon
☎ 01874 658272

Wye Valley Walk & Severn Way
For information on the above and other recreational trails, Recreational Officer:
☎ 01597 827567
www.powystrails.org.uk

Shropshire

Cycle Hire and Cycling
Cycle ride leaflets available from TICs or
☎ 01743 253008
www.shropshire.gov.uk/cycling.nsf

South Shropshire

Balloon Flights
☎ 01743 790100
www.espiritu-balloonflights.co.uk

Guided Walking Breaks
☎ 01694 723600
www.secrethillswalking.co.uk

Ludlow Guided Walks
☎ 01584 874205
Apr-Oct, Sat-Sun, BH Mon; 2.30pm from the cannon by the castle

Events

Herefordshire

Bishop Castle Agricultural Show – last Sat in July
☎ 01588 630070
Also Michaelmas Fair, usually 3rd weekend in Sep

Clun Greenman Festival – 3 days in May
Info/Bookings ☎ 01588 640305
info@clungreenman.org.uk

Hay Festival – May
☎ 0870 990 1299
www.hayfestival.co.uk

Kington Festival – June
☎ 01544 231209
www.kingtonfestival.co.uk

Kington Show – September
☎ 01544 260602
www.kingtonshow.co.uk

Leominster Festival – June
☎ 01568 611553

Monmouthshire

Abergavenny Food Festival – September
☎ 01873 851643
www.abergavennyfoodfestival.com

Monmouth Country Show
Monmouth Showground, off A466
Monmouth-Chepstow road
☎ 01283 820548

Powys

Welsh Food Festival – Glansevern Hall &
Gardens, Nr Welshpool, September
☎ 01686 640916

Brecon Food Festival – October
www.getactive-beacons.co.uk

Brecon Jazz – August
☎ 01874 611622
www.breconjazz.co.uk

Builth Wells

Royal Welsh Show – July
☎ 01982 554406

Mid Wales Mouthful Food Festival
– April
Royal Welsh Showground
☎ 01982 552224
www.wonderwoolwales.co.uk/mouthful

Presteigne

Festival of Music – August
☎ 01544 267800
www.presteignefestival.com
Please check: details subject to change

Herefordshire Cider

Although there is a Cider Trail in the county, over half of it is east of the River Wye and therefore well away from the Welsh Borders. This list of producers covers those to the west of that river and starts with the Hereford Cider Museum and then works from the south in a northwards direction.

Brook Farm Cider
Wigmore, Leominster HR6 9UJ

Dunkertons Cider Co
Luntley, Pembridge, Leominster HR6 9ED
☎ 01544 388653

Gwatkin Cider
Moorhampton Farm (some literature
states Abbey Dore Farm Shop)
Abbey Dore HR2 0AL
☎ 01981 550258
Award winning cider and perry from a
well-stocked farm shop

Hereford Cider Museum
21 Ryelands St, Hereford
☎ 01432 354207
Learn the history of cider production
before setting off!

Newton Court Cider
Newton, Leominster HR6 0PF
☎ 01568 611721

Orgasmic Cider Co
Gt Parton, Eardisley HR3 6NX
☎ 01544 327244

Ross-on-Wye Cider & Perry Co Ltd
Broome Farm, Peterstow LR9 6QG
☎ 01989 567232

Tourist Information

Abergavenny
Swan Meadow
☎ 01873 857588

Brecon
Market carpark
☎ 01874 622485

Builth Wells
Groe St carpark
☎ 01982 553307

Chepstow
Castle carpark
☎ 01291 623772

Coleford
High St
☎ 01594 812388

Crickhowell
Beaufort St
☎ 01873 812105

Hay-on-Wye
Oxford St
☎ 01497 820144

Hereford
1 King St
☎ 01432 268430

Kington
2 Mill St
☎ 01544 230778

Knighton
West St
☎ 01547 528753

Leominster
1 Corn Sq
☎ 01568 616460

Llandrindod Wells
Princes Ave
☎ 01597 822600

Ludlow
Castle Sq
☎ 01584 813666

Newent
7 Church St
☎ 01531 822468

Presteigne
Broad St ☎ 01544 260650

Queenswood
(nr Hereford) Country Park
☎ 01568 797842

Ross-on-Wye
Edde Cross St
☎ 01989 562768

Visiting Gardens

Gloucestershire

Cyril Hart Arboretum – see p.68

Lydney Park Spring Gardens – see pp.64, 69

Herefordshire

Abbey Dore Court – Abbey Dore

Berrington Court (NT) – see pp.17, 32

Blackfriars Rose Garden – Hereford – see pp. 25, 34

Croft Castle (NT) – see pp.16, 18, 32

Hampton Court – Hope under Dinmore – see pp.24, 27, 33

Hergest Croft Gardens, Kington – see p.33

Queenswood Arboretum – nr Leominster – see p.33

The Weir Garden (NT) – Swainshill, Hereford

Westonbury Mill Water Gardens – Pembridge – see p.33

Monmouthshire

Dewstow Gardens & Grottoes – Caerwent – see p.67

High Glanau Manor – Lydart

☎ 01600 860005
Open: by appointment May-Sep. Arts & Crafts Garden

Linda Vista Gardens – Abergavenny – see p.88

Penpergwm Lodge – Abergavenny – see p.88

The Nurtons – Tintern – see p.67

Veddw House – Devauden, nr Chepstow – see p.67

Wyndcliffe Court – St Arvans, Chepstow
☎ 01291 627597
By appointment, Arts & Crafts Garden

Powys

Glan Severn Hall & Gardens – Berriew
☎ 01686 640916

The Hall at Abbey-Cwm-Hir – see p.49

Whimble Nursery/Gardens – Kennerton
LD8 2PD – see p.50

Farmers' Markets

Herefordshire
Great Malvern
Near the abbey, 3rd Sat of month

Hay on Wye
Broad St, every Thurs

Hereford
Market Pantry, High Town, 1st Sat of month

Leominster
Corn Sq, 2nd Sat of month

Ross on Wye
1st Fri of month 9am-1pm

Monmouthshire
Abergavenny
Market Hall, Torfaen
☎ 0845610 6496
4th Thurs in month, 9.30am-2.30pm

Brecon
Market Hall
2nd Sat monthly, 10am-2pm

Chepstow
Senior Citizens Centre, Cormeilles Sq
☎ 01291 627416

Monmouth
Monnow Medieval Bridge
☎ 0845 6106496
4th Sat in month, 10am-1pm

Usk
Maryport St, Usk
☎ 0845 6106496
1st & 3rd Sat in month, 10am-1pm

Powys
Knighton Community Centre
Powys
4th Sat monthly 10am-1pm

Llandrindod Wells
Middleton St, Powys
Last Thurs in month, 9am-1pm

Rhayader
The Smithfield
2nd Thurs in month

Shropshire
Craven Arms
Discovery Centre
☎ 01588 676000
1st Sat of month, 9am-2pm

Ludlow
Castle Sq
2nd Thurs

Index

Published in the UK by
Landmark Publishing Ltd,
The Oaks, Moor Farm Road West, Ashbourne, DE6 1HD
Tel: 01335 347349 website: landmarkpublishing.co.uk

ISBN: 978-1-84306-445-9

British Library Cataloguing in Publication Data: a catalogue record for this book is available
from the British Library.

Print: Gutenberg Press Ltd, Malta

Front cover: Gatehouse at Stokesay Castle
Back Cover top: The Old House, Hereford
Back Cover middle: Royal Welsh Show, Builth Wells
Back Cover bottom: Raglan Castle
Back Cover bottom-right: The road bridge at Chepstow

Picture Credits

Reproduced by kind permission of the Dean and Chapter of Hereford: p.26
The Royal Welsh Agricultural Society: p.43
Cadw, Welsh Assembly Government (Crown Copyright):
p.58 top right and p.78 bottom 3 photos
Clearwell Caves: p.63 & inset
Chris Gilbert: p.27 top, p.54 bottom & inset

Images below are from Shutterstock with copyright to:
David Hughes: front cover p.6, p.10, p.11, p.39 bottom
Stephen Aaron Rees: p.39 middle **Lukáš Hejtman:** p.62

Other photography by Lindsey Porter